500 PITCHERS

500 PITCHERS

Contemporary Expressions of a Classic Form

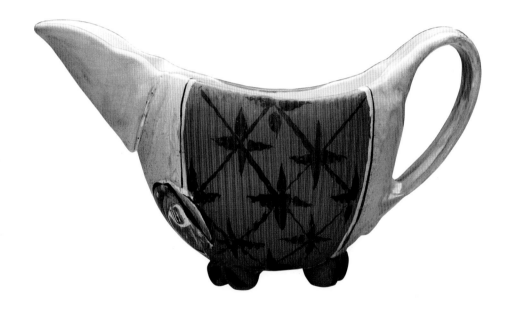

LARK BOOKS

A Division of Sterling Publishing Co., Inc.
New York

Library of Congress Cataloging-in-Publication Data

500 pitchers : contemporary expressions of a classic form / editor: Suzanne
J.E. Tourtillott.-- 1st ed.
    p. cm.
  Includes index.
  ISBN 1-57990-687-7 (pbk.)
  1. Pitchers--United States--Catalogs. 2. Pottery, American--21st
century--Catalogs. I. Tourtillott, Suzanne J. E. II. Title: Five hundred
pitchers.
NK4695.P5A15 2006
738'.0973--dc22

                        2005024927

10 9 8 7 6 5 4 3 2 1

First Edition

Published by Lark Books, A Division of
Sterling Publishing Co., Inc.
387 Park Avenue South, New York, N.Y. 10016

© 2006, Lark Books

Distributed in Canada by Sterling Publishing,
c/o Canadian Manda Group, 165 Dufferin Street
Toronto, Ontario, Canada M6K 3H6

Distributed in the United Kingdom by GMC Distribution Services,
Castle Place, 166 High Street, Lewes, East Sussex, England BN7 1XU

Distributed in Australia by Capricorn Link (Australia) Pty Ltd.,
P.O. Box 704, Windsor, NSW 2756 Australia

If you have questions or comments about this book, please contact:
Lark Books
67 Broadway
Asheville, NC 28801
(828) 253-0467

Manufactured in China

ISBN 13: 978-1-57990-687-0
ISBN 10: 1-57990-687-7

For information about custom editions, special sales, premium and corporate
purchases, please contact Sterling Special Sales Department at 800-805-5489 or
specialsales@sterlingpub.com.

EDITOR
Suzanne J.E. Tourtillott

ART DIRECTOR
Kristi Pfeffer

COVER DESIGNER
Barbara Zaretsky

ASSISTANT EDITORS
Rebecca Guthrie, Nathalie Mornu

ASSOCIATE ART DIRECTOR
Shannon Yokeley

ART PRODUCTION ASSISTANTS
Jeff Hamilton, Jackie Kerr

EDITORIAL ASSISTANCE
Delores Gosnell

EDITORIAL INTERNS
Metta L. Pry, David Squires

ART INTERNS
Emily Kepley, Nathan Schulman

Contents

The pitcher is an ancient, useful shape, symbolic as well as practical. It has long played a central role in the ritual and ceremonial life of civilizations worldwide. The vessel itself is often as powerful a symbol of significance and metaphor as the liquid it's meant to contain.

Yet the pitcher is also a deceivingly complicated form, full of particular challenges for the potter. Handle and spout, belly and foot all conspire to determine the practicality and personality of each unique piece. And as with any pottery, the visual and tactile qualities that the potter, the clay, and the heat contribute add immeasurably to the finished beauty and success of each pitcher.

The pitcher tradition has been deep and sustaining, with numerous avenues of custom and style, and the interplay between form and function continues to be explored today, as this remarkable collection of contemporary pitchers demonstrates so vividly. One aspect investigated by contemporary studio potters is the pitcher's communal usefulness: unlike the teacup or the coffee mug that soon becomes one person's personal favorite, the pitcher's simple purposefulness holds refreshment and service for several. Some potters also use the pitcher form as a vehicle for their considerable skill at drawing and painting, such as Rosalie Wynkoop's *Majolica Pitcher*; others view it as a means to investigate spatial relationships, as does Scott Dooley's *Zigzag Watering Can*.

Caroline Holder's *A Woman's Hair is Her Crowning Glory* is an example of how still others infuse commentary or narrative into their work.

A potter's work revolves continually around the exploration and development of form. For example, the size and placement of a pitcher's belly indicate the quantity it can hold. Adama Sow's *Shino Pitcher* is spherical and voluminous, while Do-Hee Sung's *Green Bamboo Pitcher* is based on a short, stately cylindrical form. Consider, too, the spout: it is, perhaps, a pitcher's most prominent feature. This collection includes an array of spouts, from exaggerated drama (an untitled pitcher by Lilach Lotan) to the nearly nonexistent (Lois Harbaugh's *Hollow Leg*).

Ceramics history also offers potters a rich and fertile ground for discovery and interpretation. Some artists follow the ancient path of incorporating animal imagery into utilitarian ware, as with Karen Copensky's realistic *Cape Buffalo Ewer*; others follow the equally long-standing tradition of referencing animal posture or gesture, as in the subtle poise of Michael Kline's *Pitcher*.

Whether it's a flagon reserved for sacred ceremony, a humble little oil ewer on the back of the stove, a spirited margarita pitcher, or a family heirloom filled with seasonal garden flowers, each pitcher really comes into its own when it's put into use. For instance, a

Rosalie Wynkoop, *Majolica Pitcher*

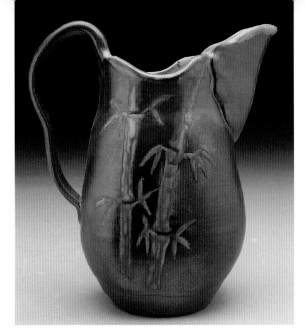

Do-Hee Sung, *Green Bamboo Pitcher*

especially interested in selecting those pitchers that seemed to possess the ability to enhance, fulfill, sustain, or comment on each potter's particular understanding of the pitcher as a cultural object of purposefulness, expression, or beauty.

I am pleased with the variety of quiet, well-designed pitchers—what some potters might refer to as "honest work"—as well as the fine examples of vigorous, sculptural pieces in this book. To add even more value, some images are accompanied by commentary, either from me or from the artist. The collection is interspersed with my insights and thoughts covering the range of themes introduced in this flourishing assortment. Sometimes I compare two pieces on the same spread; at other times, just one. Furthermore, selected remarks by the artists themselves shed light on their inspirations and working methods. May this book serve you well as inspiration, source, and refreshment!

—Terry Gess

visit to my mother's house usually includes breakfast, when she uses a small cream pitcher that I made and gave to her years ago. It's a short form, wider in the belly, with a handle rising slightly off and away from the lip and a splash of carefully placed sgrafitto. Certainly she loves it as her son's handmade gift, but her daily use of it speaks well of the lasting and endearing tradition of pitchers.

I was delighted when Lark Books asked me to review the many excellent entries for *500 Pitchers: Contemporary Expressions of a Classic Form.* With more than 4,000 images to choose from, we chose broadly, attempting to represent the wide range of style and technique that potters submitted for consideration. We were

Karen Copensky, *Cape Buffalo Ewer*

Dan Anderson

Conoco Oil Pitcher, 2004

12 x 11 x 6½ inches (30.5 x 27.9 x 16.5 cm)
Slab-built stoneware; soda fired, 1300°F (704°C);
decal fired and sandblasted
PHOTO BY JEFF BRUCE

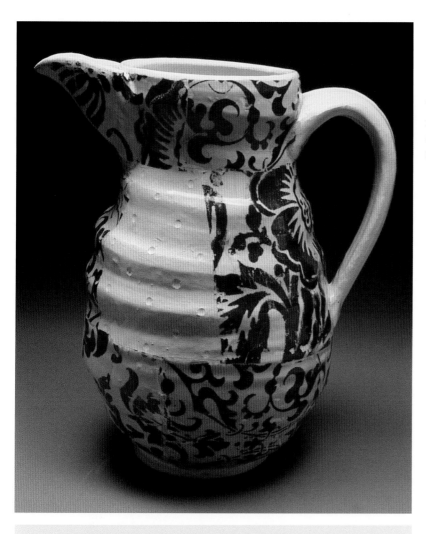

Kelly McKibben

Untitled, 2005

11 x 9½ x 7 inches (27.9 x 24.1 x 17.8 cm)
Thrown white earthenware; electric
fired, cone 04; silkscreen slips,
cone 04; clear glaze
PHOTO BY ARTIST

Kelly McKibben used at least three distinct decorative motifs, each one at certain odds with the others. This challenging approach to surface treatment has historical referents in Japanese Oribe ware. —TG

Hide Sadohara

Shino Pitcher, 1994

10 x 6 x 6 inches (25.4 x 15.2 x 15.2 cm)
Wheel-thrown and altered porcelain;
reduction fired, cone 10
PHOTO BY ARTIST

Patti Hughes

Untitled, 2002

7¼ x 5¾ x 3¾ inches (18.4 x 14.6 x 9.5 cm)
Wheel-thrown and altered stoneware;
reduction fired, cone 10
PHOTO BY TIM BARKLEY

G. Michael Davis

Grey Pitcher B2, 2005

11 x 6 x 4 inches (27.9 x 15.2 x 10.2 cm)
Porcelain; reduction fired, cone 10
PHOTO BY ARTIST

Jerry L. Bennett

I Think It's a Bird Pitcher, 2003

15 x 9 x 11 inches (38.1 x 22.9 x 27.9 cm)
Wheel-thrown and altered stoneware paper
clay; single fired in oxidation, cone 6;
slab-built additions

PHOTO BY JOHN CARLAND

Bede Clarke

Pitcher, 2003

13½ x 7 x 4 inches (34.3 x 17.8 x 10.2 cm)
Wheel-thrown stoneware; wood fired in
anagama kiln, cone 12
PHOTO BY ARTIST

Bede Clarke kept the surface of this
lean pitcher smooth and largely free
of texture so that it would be open
to the nuances of flame and ash
during firing. —_TG_

Jeff Kaller

Pitcher, 2004

10½ x 10 x 5½ inches (26.7 x 25.4 x 14 cm)
Wheel-thrown porcelain; high-fired in reduction;
clear glaze with cobalt sulfate decoration
PHOTO BY ARTIST

Sarah Raymond

Untitled, 2004

5¼ x 3½ x 3½ inches (13.3 x 8.9 x 8.9 cm)
Soft-slab stoneware; electric fired, cone 6
PHOTO BY VINCENT NOGUCHI

Anne Fallis Elliott

| *Side Handle Pitcher on a Tray*, 2003

Pitcher: 5 x 6 x 4 inches (12.7 x 15.2 x 10.2 cm)
Tray: 10 inches (25.4 cm)
Wheel-thrown, altered, and assembled stoneware;
electric fired, cone 7; ash glaze
PHOTO BY KEVIN NOBLE

Kazu Oba

Sake Pitcher, 2004

Pitcher: 3 x 6 x 5 inches (7.6 x 15.2 x 12.7 cm)
Wheel-thrown stoneware; electric fired, cone 6
PHOTO BY ARTIST

Vijay V. Paniker

Celadon Pitcher, 2005

11½ x 6½ x 8¼ inches (29.2 x 16.5 x 21 cm)
Wheel-thrown stoneware; gas fired, cone 10
PHOTOS BY ANDREA M. ALLEN

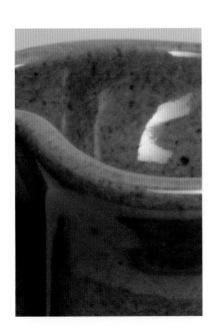

Covered Pitcher, 2004

14 x 6 inches (35.6 x 15.2 cm)
Porcelain; soda fired, cone 10; slip
PHOTO BY ARTIST

Jay Owens

Wine Carafe 3, 2005

16 x 9 x 8 inches (40.6 x 22.9 x 20.3 cm)
Wheel-thrown red earthenware;
electric fired, cone 04; white slip,
alkaline glaze, sgraffitto
PHOTO BY ARTIST

Peg Malloy

Gravy Boat, 2004

5 x 7½ x 5 inches (12.7 x 19 x 12.7 cm)
Wheel-thrown and altered white stoneware;
wood fired, cone 11; shino slip
PHOTO BY ARTIST

Aladdin's Pouring Vessel, 2004

10½ x 6½ x 3 inches (26.7 x 16.5 x 7.6 cm)
Wheel-thrown stoneware; electric fired, cone 6
PHOTO BY PETER JACOBS

Pitchers so beautifully demonstrate what dramatic differences can be made with a tiny change in the swell of the body, the placement or curve of the handle, and the size and shape of the pouring lip. —JM

Kate Biderbost

| Untitled, 2004

5 x 4 x 4 inches (12.7 x 10.2 x 10.2 cm)
Wheel-thrown stoneware; soda fired, cone 10
PHOTO BY WILLIAM BIDERBOST

Mark Fitzgerald
Untitled, 2004

10½ x 8 x 6½ inches
(26.7 x 20.3 x 16.5 cm)
Wheel-thrown stoneware; reduction
fired, cone 10; wood-ash glaze
PHOTO BY ARTIST

Larry Clegg

Untitled, 2004

10½ x 5 x 6 inches (26.7 x 12.7 x 15.2 cm)
Wheel-thrown porcelain in two sections;
electric fired, 2320°F (1271°C); incised and
impressed designs, airbrushed glazes
PHOTO BY LARRY SANDERS

Mary Beth Bishop

Friend of Winter, Plum Blossoms, 2004

5 x 3 x 3 inches (12.7 x 7.6 x 7.6 cm)
Wheel-thrown porcelain; soda fired, cone 10; layered
shino slip and glaze with wax resist and iron oxide brushed
decoration; electric fired, cone 5; overglaze decoration
PHOTOS BY YORK WILSON OF MONKEY EYE STUDIO

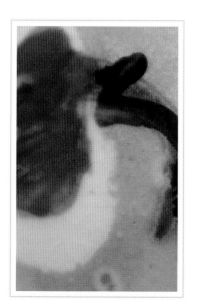

Barbara Newell

Helping Hands, 2003

12 x 14 x 14 inches (30.5 x 35.6 x 35.6 cm)
Wheel-thrown and hand-built stoneware;
wood fired, cone 10; shino glaze
PHOTO BY ARTIST

Linda McFarling

Gravy Boat, 2005

5 x 6 x 4½ inches
(12.7 x 15.2 x 11.4 cm)
Wheel-thrown and darted
stoneware; soda fired, cone 10
PHOTO BY TOM MILLS

Shane Mickey

Side-Fired Pitcher, 2005

15 x 8 x 7 inches (38.1 x 20.3 x 17.8 cm)
Wheel-thrown stoneware; anagama fired
PHOTO BY TOM MILLS

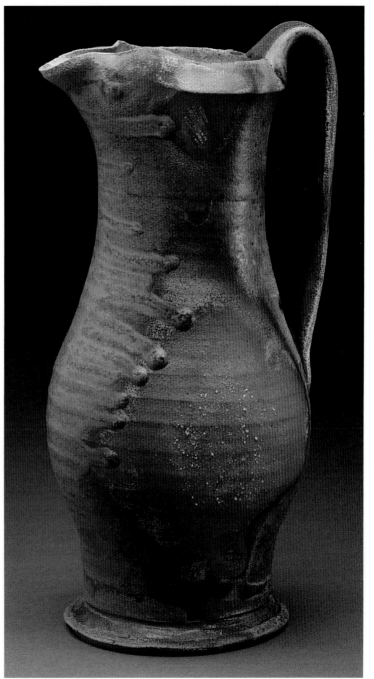

Elisabeth Ottebring

Pink Pitcher, 2005

7¹/₁₆ x 5³/₁₆ x 3⁷/₈ (18 x 13 x 10 cm)
Wheel-thrown porcelain with press-
molded details; oxidation fired, cone 8;
underglazes, silkscreen transfers
PHOTO BY PER KRISTIANSEN

Rachelle Chinnery

Wind over Water, 2004

6 x 2¾ x 4 inches (15.2 x 7 x 10.2 cm)
Wheel-thrown, altered, and carved
porcelain; electric fired, cone 6
PHOTO BY KEN MAYER

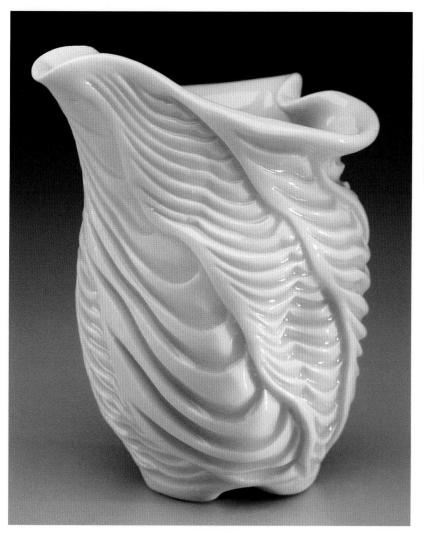

A handle-less pitcher
suggests small scale and
great intimacy. Rachelle
Chinnery adds to that
effect with the deeply
contoured tactile surface
of her piece. —*TG*

Michèle C. Drivon

Gravy Boat, 2005

6¾ x 5¼ x 3½ inches (17.1 x 13.3 x 8.3 cm)
Wheel-thrown and altered porcelain; gas fired
in reduction, cone 10
PHOTO BY ARTIST

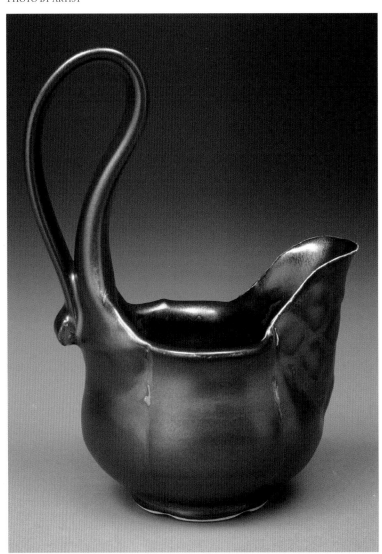

Kevin DeKeuster

Untitled, 1999

12 x 9½ x 7½ inches
(30.5 x 24.1 x 19 cm)
Wheel-thrown stoneware;
wood fired, cone 12
PHOTO BY ARTIST

John Arnold Taylor

Small Pitcher—Little Guy, 2005

6 x 5 x 4 inches (15.2 x 12.7 x 10.2 cm)
Wheel-thrown stoneware; electric fired,
cone 6; slips, stains, underglaze, and glaze
PHOTO BY ARTIST

David Lloyd Warren

Calypso Pitcher #3, 2004

13 x 6½ x 2¾ inches (33 x 16.5 x 7 cm)
Hand-built low-fire clay; electric fired, cone 06
PHOTO BY ARTIST

With a wide range of influences, from nature to architecture, my ceramics explore the sculptural possibilities of utilitarian objects. My intent is to investigate the complexities of form and surface and to create pieces that engage the mind and heart, pushing the boundaries of functionalism and art. My interest is primarily in the ambiguities of form and the functional illusions that surface treatment makes possible. —*DLW*

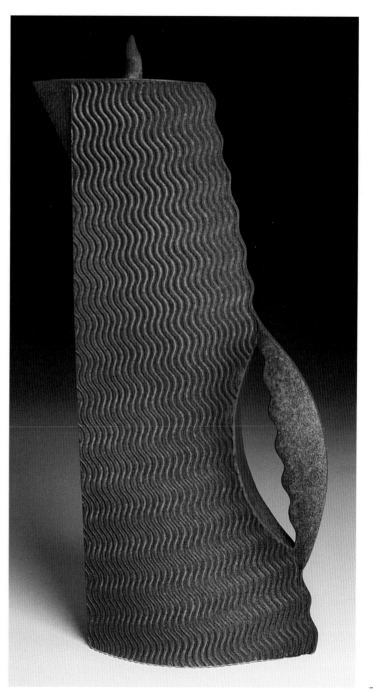

Heather Newman

Crossing the Line Pouring Pitcher, 2005

9½ x 7 x 6½ inches (24.1 x 17.8 x 16.5 cm)
Stoneware; gas fired in reduction; shino,
layered glazes
PHOTO BY STEVE MANN

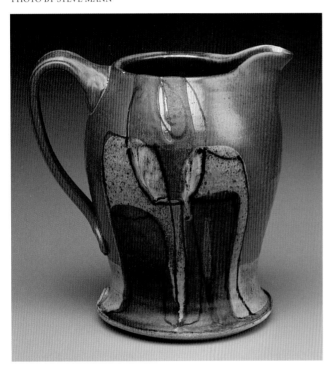

Amy Sanders

Untitled, 2004

8 x 8 x 4 inches (20.3 x 20.3 x 10.2 cm)
Wheel-thrown, altered, stamped, and
assembled stoneware; electric fired, cone 6;
layered oxides and glazes
PHOTO BY SHANE BASKIN

Jenny Lou Sherburne

Quart Pitcher, 1993

11 x 7 x 5½ inches (27.9 x 17.8 x 14 cm)
Wheel-thrown and altered earthenware;
electric fired, cones 4 to 6; carved
with applied textures, engobes,
and colored glazes
PHOTO BY GUY NICHOLS

Stephen Driver

North Coast Ghost Series:
Heron Effigy, 2002

12½ x 11 x 4½ inches
(31.8 x 27.9 x 11.4 cm)
Slab-built and press-molded
porcelain; wood fired, cone 12
PHOTO BY GEORGE CHAMBERS

Joanne Taylor Brown

Flora and Fauna Pitcher, 2004

11 x 7 x 7 inches (27.9 x 17.8 x 17.8 cm)
Slab-built porcelain; reduction fired,
cone 10; celadon glaze
PHOTO BY JOHN CARLANO

Joanne Taylor Brown and Stephen Driver offer two variations on the animistic avenue of pitchers. Past cultures provide many examples of ritual ewers and pitchers that incorporate the long neck and beak of an aviary creature; some pitchers replicate entire animals. —*TG*

Francisco Dozier

Untitled, 2005

8½ x 5 x 11½ inches (21.6 x 12.7 x 29.2 cm)
Wheel-thrown earthenware; electric fired,
cone 06; underglazes, cone 06; acrylic paint
PHOTO BY ARTIST

Sharon Woodward

Mardi Gras Bird, 2005

8 1/4 x 7 x 4 inches (21 x 17.8 x 10.2 cm)
Hand-built porcelain; transparent glaze over
underglazes, cone 6; gold lustre, cone 017
PHOTO BY ARTIST

Gabriel Kline

Sugarmint Pitcher, 2005

10 x 7 x 7 inches
(25.4 x 17.8 x 17.8 cm)
Wheel-thrown white stoneware;
electric fired in oxidation, cone 7;
dipped and sprayed glazes
PHOTO BY RYAN PHILLIPS

Daniel Crump

Pitcher, 2004

12 x 6 x 6 inches (30.5 x 15.2 x 15.2 cm)
Wheel-thrown stoneware; salt fired, cone 10
PHOTO BY SUSAN D. HARRIS

Our vocabulary hints at our affection for pitchers; we speak of them in anthropomorphic terms: foot, belly, spout, lip. Daniel Crump offers for our examination an elegant anatomical model, stripped of all but the subtlest adornment. —TG

Joanne Taylor Brown

Pitcher, 2004

10 x 6 x 6 inches (25.4 x 15.2 x 15.2 cm)
Slab-built porcelain; reduction fired, cone 10;
celadon glaze interior, unglazed exterior
PHOTO BY JOHN CARLANO

Sylvia Ramachandran

Ferocious Cub, 2003

7 x 5½ x 2½ inches (17.8 x 14 x 6.4 cm)
Slab-built and carved earthenware; multiple
electric firings, cones 04 to 06; commercial
underglazes, matte glaze
PHOTO BY DAVID HAWKINSON

Mark Issenberg

Ash-Glazed Stoneware Pitcher, 2004

9 x 7 inches (22.9 x 17.8 cm)
Wheel-thrown stoneware; reduction
fired in gas kiln, cone 10; ash glazes
PHOTO BY NORTHLIGHT IMAGING SERVICES

Eloise Hally

Shino Pitcher, 2004

12 x 6 x 5 inches (30.5 x 15.2 x 12.7 cm)
Wheel-thrown stoneware; gas fired in
reduction, cone 10; shino glaze, iron
oxide and engobe overglaze brushwork
PHOTO BY BART KASTEN

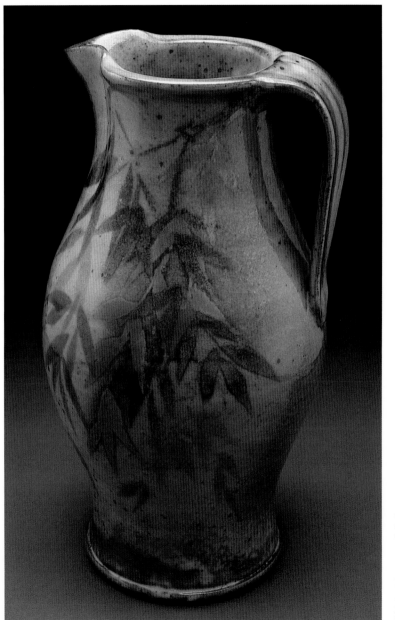

Paul F. Morris

Corpulent Greed Ewer, 2004

30½ x 10½ x 15¾ inches (77.5 x 26.7 x 40 cm)
Hand-built earthenware; multiple electric firings,
cones 04 to 014

PHOTO BY ARTIST

Meira Mathison

Sherry Set for My English Neighbor, 2004

Pitcher: 6 x 3½ inches (15.2 x 8.9 cm)
Cups: 3 x 2 inches (7.6 x 5 cm)
Tray: 8 x 6 inches (20.3 x 15.2 cm)
Wheel-thrown and altered porcelain; reduction fired, cone 10;
stamped and colored clay sprigs; multi-layered glaze
PHOTO BY JANET DWYER

Sandra Black

Ripple Jugs: Series Two, 2003

Left: 2 x 2 inches (5 x 5 cm)
Right: 2¾ x 2¼ inches (7 x 5.76 cm)
Wheel-thrown Southern Ice porcelain;
gas fired in reduction, cone 10; satin white glaze
PHOTO BY VICTOR FRANCE
COURTESY OF PERTH GALLERIES

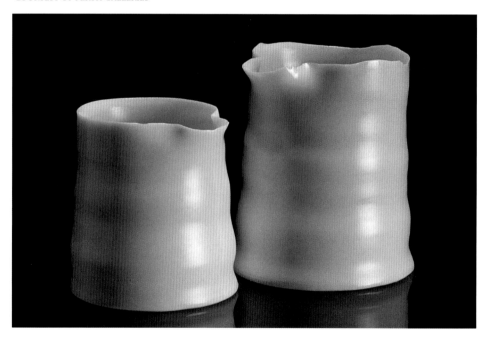

Journeys to both Canada and Japan have exposed me to water in all its forms—as snow, ice, glaciers, and melt water, either flowing or contained in lakes. I observed how it is used, contained, and ritualized. From these experiences, I've tried to distill elements that suggest the forms of water, its movement in response to landscape and atmospheric events, and how we contain and consume it. —SB

Johanna DeMay
Will DeMay

Carved Pitcher, 2005

12½ inches tall (31.8 cm)
Wheel-thrown, altered, and
assembled stoneware;
reduction fired, cone 10;
brushwork and carving
PHOTO BY MARGOT GEIST

Marty Fielding

| *Pitcher,* 2005

10 x 7½ x 6 inches (25.4 x 19 x 15.2 cm)
Wheel-thrown stoneware; reduction fired,
cone 10; layered glazes
PHOTO BY ARTIST

Michéle C. Drivon

| *Lady Pitcher,* 2004

12 x 6 x 4¼ inches (30.5 x 15.2 x 10.8 cm)
Wheel-thrown and altered porcelain;
electric fired, cone 6
PHOTO BY ARTIST

Kathryne Koop

Untitled, 2004

15¾ x 7½ x 4½ inches (40 x 19 x 11.4 cm)
Wheel-thrown porcelain; gas fired in
reduction, cone 11

PHOTO BY BRUCE SPIELMAN

Mark Johnson

Pouring Vessel, 2004

14 x 10 x 8 inches (35.6 x 25.4 x 20.3 cm)
Wheel-thrown and altered white
stoneware; soda fired, cone 10;
glaze, cone 10
PHOTO BY ARTIST

I enjoy the
challenge of
making a vessel
that pours well,
fits the hand,
and possesses a
confident form.

—*MJ*

Vijay V. Paniker

Antique Pitcher, 2005

14¼ x 7 x 8½ inches (36.2 x 17.8 x 21.6 cm)
Wheel-thrown stoneware; gas fired, cone 10
PHOTO BY ANDREA M. ALLEN

Fleur Schell

Porcelain Gravy Jug, 2003

6¼ x 3½ x 3½ inches (16 x 9 x 9 cm)
Wheel-thrown and assembled porcelain using
textured slabs and coils; electric fired, cone 8
PHOTO BY ADRIAN LAMBERT

Nigel Rudolph

Lidded Pitcher, 2004

7½ x 6 x 4½ inches (19 x 15.2 x 11.4 cm)
Wheel-thrown porcelain; reduction fired
with soda, cone 11

PHOTOS BY ARTIST

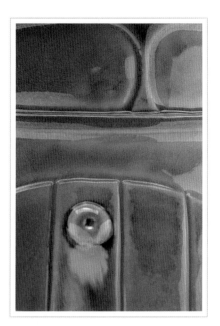

Markus Urbanik

Carved Celadon Pitcher, 2004

12 x 8 x 7 inches (30.5 x 20.3 x 17.8 cm)
Wheel-thrown porcelain; gas fired, cone 10
PHOTO BY ARTIST

Sandy Kinzie

Untitled, 2004

9 x 6 x 1½ inches (22.9 x 15.2 x 3.8 cm)
Wheel-thrown, textured, and hand-built
stoneware; reduction fired, cone 10
PHOTO BY ARTIST

Frank James Fisher

Milk Pitcher, 2005

10½ x 3½ x 6 inches (26.7 x 8.9 x 15.2 cm)
Slab-built porcelain; raku fired
PHOTOS BY ARTIST

Michael T. Schmidt

*Shell Pitcher, Chevron Funnel,
and Base,* 2005

7 x 10 x 7 inches (17.8 x 25.4 x 17.8 cm)
Earthenware and slip-cast porcelain;
multi-fired; digital image transfer
PHOTO BY ARTIST

Untitled, 2004

12 x 7 x 6 inches (30.5 x 17.8 x 15.2 cm)
Slab-built stoneware; soda fired, cone 10
PHOTO BY ARTIST

Matt Kelleher's fine
pitcher is composed of
simple, well-executed
shapes. His direct
approach to construction
instills this piece with
stature and confidence.

—TG

Posey Bacopoulos

Beaked Pitcher, 2003

8 x 8½ x 3½ inches (20.3 x 21.6 x 8.9 cm)
Thrown, altered, and assembled terra cotta;
electric fired, cone 04; majolica
PHOTO BY KEVIN NOBLE

The floral motifs on my pots
are patterns rather than
actual representations. They
serve to divide the space in
interesting ways. —*PB*

Michèle C. Drivon

Gravy Boat and Saucer, 2004

6¼ x 6¼ x 5¾ inches (15.9 x 15.9 x 14.6 cm)
Wheel-thrown and altered porcelain; electric
fired, cone 6; celadon glaze
PHOTO BY ARTIST

Felicia Breen

Beetle Pitcher II, 2004

12 x 9 x 6 inches (30.5 x 22.9 x 15.2 cm)
Wheel-thrown and altered white
stoneware; salt fired, cone 10
PHOTOS BY ARTIST

Ellen Shankin

Squared Creamer, 2004

6 x 4 x 4 inches (15.2 x 10.2 x 10.2 cm)
Wheel-thrown and altered stoneware;
reduction fired, cone 10; crystal matte glaze

PHOTO BY TIM BARNWELL

Bradley C. Birkhimer

| Untitled, 2005

9½ x 5½ x 5 inches (24.1 x 14 x 12.7 cm)
Wheel-thrown porcelain; wood and soda
fired, cone 11
PHOTO BY ARTIST

Wynne Wilbur

Neutral, Ripe, 2004

7 x 6 x 4 inches (17.8 x 15.2 x 10.2 cm)
Wheel-thrown and altered terra cotta;
electric fired, cone 03; majolica
PHOTO BY ARTIST

Lauren Kearns

Untitled, 2001–2002

12 x 7 inches (30.5 x 17.8 cm)
Hand-thrown porcelain; electric fired,
cone 9; hand-painted gold luster
PHOTO BY LYNN THOMPSON

Angela Walford

Black Pitcher, 2003

8¼ x 5⅛ inches (21 x 13 cm)
Wheel-thrown, altered, and slip cast
Walker No. 10 stoneware; reduction
fired, cone 9; black engobe
PHOTO BY ARTIST

I'm often captivated by pottery forms that move outside the box—that appear to take their inspiration or reference from some source other than the mainstream of ceramic history. Angela Walford presents us with such a form, perhaps modeled after a shell or pod that she has reduced to basic volumes. —*TG*

Vijay V. Paniker

Bamboo Pitcher, 2005

9¾ x 4 x 7½ inches (24.8 x 10.2 x 19 cm)
Wheel-thrown stoneware; gas fired, cone 10
PHOTOS BY ANDREA M. ALLEN

Jeff Kaller

Pitcher, 2004

10 x 9 x 5 inches (25.4 x 22.9 x 12.7 cm)
Wheel-thrown porcelain; high-fired in reduction;
clear glaze with cobalt sulfate decoration
PHOTO BY ARTIST

Gary Georger

| *Pitcher*, 2004

9 x 5½ inches (22.9 x 14 cm)
Wheel-thrown stoneware;
wood fired, cone 10;
altered, temmoku
PHOTO BY ARTIST

Judith Duff

| *Pitcher*, 2004

6 x 4 x 3 inches (15.2 x 10.2 x 7.6 cm)
Wheel-thrown and altered porcelain;
tumble stacked wood fired, cone 12;
natural ash glaze
PHOTO BY TOM MILLS

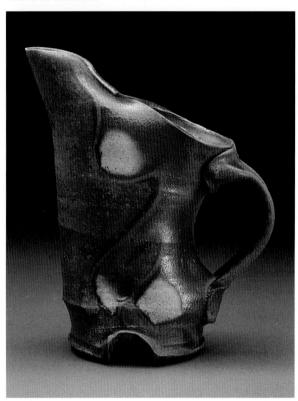

John W. Hopkins

Untitled, 2005

13 x 6 x 6 inches (33 x 15.2 x 15.2 cm)
Wheel-thrown porcelain; underglaze
slip with chattering; reduction fired,
cone 10; layered glazes

PHOTO BY ARTIST

Gary Georger

Water Jug, 2004

12 x 8 inches (30.5 x 20.3 cm)
Wheel-thrown stoneware;
wood fired, cone 10; carbon
trap shino, slip
PHOTO BY ARTIST

I use line, gesture,
and movement in clay
to allow it to speak
and to retain the
sense of a fresh, alive,
and wet pot. —GG

Nicholas Seidner

Pitcher, 2004

11 x 6 x 6 inches (27.9 x 15.2 x 15.2 cm)
Wheel-thrown stoneware; gas fired with
salt and soda, cone 10
PHOTO BY ARTIST

Gabriel Kline

Skyscraper Pitcher, 2004

24 x 8 x 8 inches (61 x 20.3 x 20.3 cm)
Wheel-thrown and assembled stoneware;
gas fired in reduction, cone 10; dipped,
trailed, and sprayed glazes
PHOTOS BY RYAN PHILLIPS

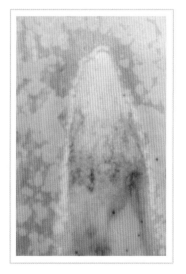

Colin Johnson

Platypus Pitcher, 2001

10 x 5 inches (25.4 x 12.7 cm)
Wheel-thrown white earthenware with
pulled handle and molded spout; electric fired, cone 5; matte opaque glaze
PHOTOS BY ARTIST

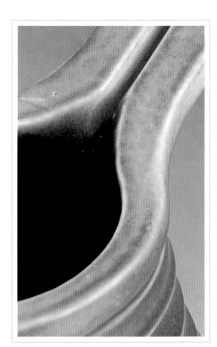

Kathryne Koop

| *Oval Pitcher,* 2004

6½ x 6½ x 3 inches (16.5 x 16.5 x 7.6 cm)
Wheel-thrown and altered porcelain; gas
fired in reduction, cone 11
PHOTO BY BRUCE SPIELMAN

Liz de Beer

| Untitled, 2004

9½ inches (24.1 cm)
Wheel-thrown porcelain; electric fired,
cone 06; matte white, cream, and
charcoal glazes, cone 04
PHOTO BY JAN DE BEER

Jason Bohnert

Pitcher, 2005

13 x 6 x 7 inches (33 x 15.2 x 17.8 cm)
Wheel-thrown, faceted, and altered white
stoneware; wood and soda fired, cone 11
PHOTO BY ARTIST

Stephen Horn

Quatrefoiled Pitcher with Appliqué, 2002

11¾ x 8¾ x 6⅜ inches (29.9 x 22.2 x 16.2 cm)
Wheel-thrown white stoneware; gas fired, cone 5
PHOTO BY JOHN HOPKINS

Lana Heckendorn

Pitcher, 2005

10 x 8 x 5 inches (25.4 x 20.3 x 12.7 cm)
Wheel-thrown, assembled, and carved
porcelain; gas fired in reduction, cone 10
PHOTO BY JOHN CARLANO

Darrell Finnegan

Plump Pitcher, 2004

9 x 9 x 7 inches (22.9 x 22.9 x 17.8 cm)
Wheel-thrown and altered stoneware;
bisque fired, cone 06; glaze, cone 6
oxidation; faux celadon glaze over
black slip and underglaze blush
PHOTO BY STEVE GYURINA

Form is most important to me. I enjoy a visual journey down the line of
a rim and over the sensuous curve of a handle, ending with a glaze that
accentuates the form. I strive for unity. —*DF*

Syrup Pitcher, 2003

5 x 6 x 4 inches
(12.7 x 15.2 x 10.2 cm)
Wheel-thrown porcelain;
reduction fired, cone 10
PHOTO BY ARTIST

This semi-transparent glaze has been kind to Steven Godfrey's pitcher.
He carved deeply into its surface, anticipating that the glaze would
pool and darken the relief's recesses and ledges. —*TG*

Ardis A. Bourland

Textured Pitcher, 2001

10 x 9 x 3 inches
(25.4 x 22.9 x 7.6 cm)
Slab-built stoneware; gas fired
in reduction; engobe; clear
overglaze, cone 10
PHOTO BY FAREED AL MASHAT

Sam Scott

Porcelain Pitcher, 2004

9 x 5½ inches (22.9 x 14 cm)
Wheel-thrown kai porcelain; gas fired in reduction,
cone 12; poured black matte and clear glazes
PHOTO BY TOM HOLT

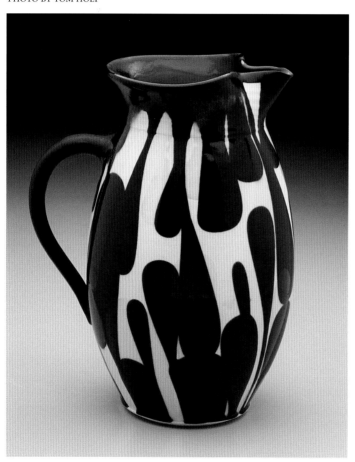

Sam Scott uses black drips to add graphic tension to his pitcher. These marks flow from both the rim and the foot, successfully unifying the overall design. —*TG*

Gillian McMillan

Pipkin with Three Tumblers, 1996

Pitcher: 12 x 8 x 5 inches (30.5 x 20.3 x 12.7 cm)
Cups: 5 x 3 inches in diameter (12.7 x 7.6)
Wheel-thrown and assembled earthenware;
electric fired, cone 04; slip painted, clear glaze
PHOTOS BY KEN MAYER

Dan Anderson

Jug, 1991

14 x 10 x 8 inches (35.6 x 25.4 x 20.3 cm)
Wheel-thrown stoneware; electric fired,
cone 06; crackle pattern glaze
PHOTO BY JOSEPH GRUBER

Chris Alexiades

Untitled, 2004

10 x 7¼ x 8 inches (25.4 x 18.4 x 20.3 cm)
Wheel-thrown stoneware; wood fired,
cone 10; clear glaze
PHOTO BY CRAIG PHILLIPS

Pouring vessels are as much functional tableware as they are figurative studies. Pitchers investigate gesture and form. My pieces have a physical presence. They speak amongst themselves and to the space around them. —CA

Jayson Lawfer

Untitled, 2003

13 x 9 x 7 inches (33 x 22.9 x 17.8 cm)
Wheel-thrown porcelain; reduction
fired with soda, cone 10
PHOTO BY CHRIS AUTIO

Bayard Morgan

Untitled, 2004

11 x 5 x 6 inches (27.9 x 12.7 x 15.2 cm)
Wheel-thrown stoneware; gas fired in
reduction, cone 10
PHOTO BY PETER LEE

Ellen Shankin

Twisted Pitcher, 2004

11 x 7 x 7 inches (27.9 x 17.8 x 17.8 cm)
Wheel-thrown and altered stoneware;
reduction fired, cone 10; fake ash glaze
PHOTO BY TIM BARNWELL

Richard Burkett

Spouted Pitcher, 2003

11 x 9 x 7 inches
(27.9 x 22.9 x 17.8 cm)
Wheel-thrown stoneware; anagama
fired with soda; natural ash glaze
PHOTO BY ARTIST

Gertrude Graham Smith

Gravy Boat, 2004

4½ x 6 inches (11.4 x 15.2 cm)
Wheel-thrown and altered porcelain;
single fired in soda kiln, cone 10
PHOTO BY TOM MILLS

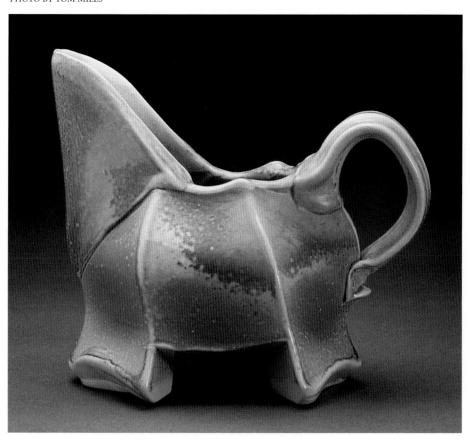

These days, I contemplate the relevance of living as a practicing artist in a world torn by conflict and exploited for resources. Working for many years as a potter develops qualities that I must believe are of benefit: caring attention, dedication, honesty, courage, passion, hard work, commitment to beauty, and a willingness to get one's hands dirty. —GGS

Juanita Disher

Untitled, 2005

9 x 5½ x 3½ inches (22.9 x 14 x 8.9 cm)
Slab-built stoneware; reduction fired, cone 10
PHOTO BY SCOTT LYKENS

Bradley C. Birkhimer

Untitled, 2005

8 x 7 x 7 inches (20.3 x 17.8 x 17.8 cm)
Wheel-thrown porcelain; wood fired, cone 11;
multiple shino glaze applications
PHOTO BY ARTIST

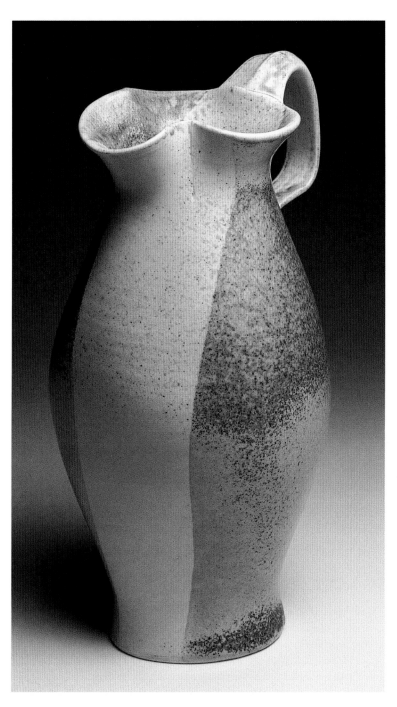

Brooke Evans

Untitled, 2004

11 x 7 x 6 inches (27.9 x 17.8 x 15.2 cm)
Porcelain; wood fired; shino glaze
PHOTO BY MARC RUSSELL

Leena Batra

Blue Pitcher, 2005

14 x 9 x 9 inches (35.6 x 22.9 x 22.9 cm)
Wheel-thrown and assembled stoneware;
gas fired, cone 9; crawled glaze
PHOTO BY HARRY KUMAR

Bob Chance

For Billy, 2004

17 x 11 inches (43.2 x 27.9 cm)
Wheel-thrown stoneware; wood
fired, cone 9; ash glaze, trailed slip,
and glass drips
PHOTO BY ARTIST

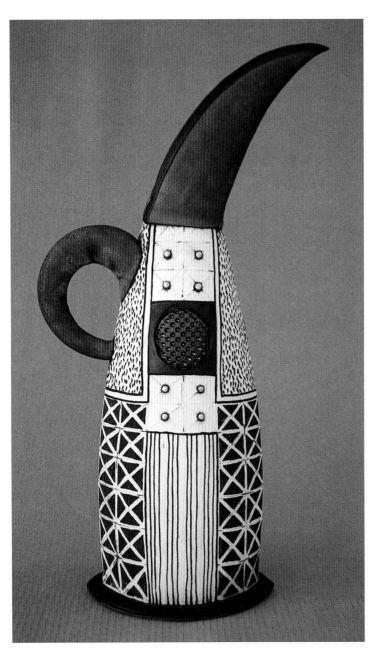

Hennie Meyer

Jug II, 2005

20 x 11½ x 5½ inches (51 x 30 x 14 cm)
Slab-built earthenware; electric fired,
cone 1; slip, glaze, oxide, and gold luster
PHOTOS BY ARTIST

Michael T. Schmidt

Texaco Pitcher, Funnel, and Base, 2005

12 x 10 x 10 inches (30.5 x 25.4 x 25.4 cm)
Earthenware and slip-cast porcelain; multi-fired;
digital image transfer
PHOTOS BY ARTIST

Sam Scott

Porcelain Pitcher, 2004

8 x 6 inches (20.3 x 15.2 cm)
Wheel-thrown kai porcelain; gas fired in reduction,
cone 12; clear glaze with overglaze brushwork
PHOTO BY TOM HOLT

The restrained, fluid brushwork on this piece flows around the form, encompassing the surface into an integrated whole. —*ss*

David Orser

｜ *Jug,* 2005

9 x 6 x 5 inches (22.9 x 15.2 x 12.7 cm)
Wheel-thrown stoneware; gas fired,
cone 10; ash glaze
PHOTO BY ARTIST

There is a beautiful, rugged
aesthetic in David Orser's
pitcher that suggests a long-ago
time when pots were simple
and unpretentious. In reality the
rough clay body, ribbon-like
handle, and his apparent
appreciation of accidental
ash-flow catching on the ledge
of the foot all indicate a consid-
ered eye and refined style. —TG

Geoff Pickett

Untitled, 2004

14 x 9 x 9 inches
(35.6 x 22.9 x 22.9 cm)
Wheel-thrown and pulled
white stoneware; wood fired,
cone 10; salt and iron glazes
PHOTO BY WALKER MONTGOMERY

Peg Malloy

Untitled, 2004

9¼ x 9 x 6 inches (23.5 x 22.9 x 15.2 cm)
Wheel-thrown and altered white stoneware;
wood fired, cone 11; shino glaze, slip
PHOTO BY ARTIST

Peg Malloy's pitcher rises up and out into space from a small, secure foot. The lift is dramatized by the vertical marks that terminate in a scalloped lip, and the entire piece moves from quiet beginnings to fluid termination. —*TG*

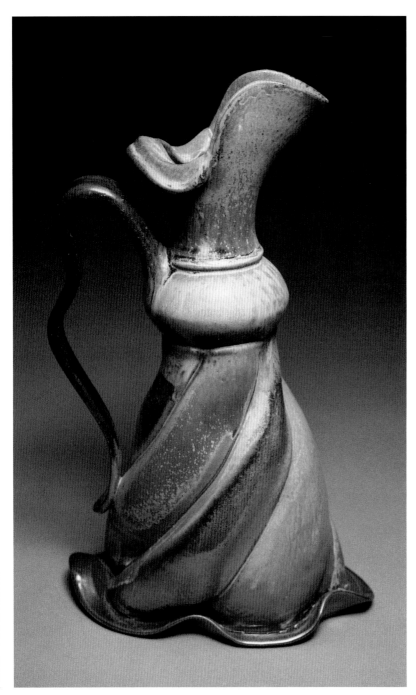

Steve Loucks

*Spiral Pitcher with Wavy
Oval Bottom,* 2004

16 x 9 x 6 inches (40.6 x 22.9 x 15.2 cm)
Wheel-thrown, altered, and assembled
white stoneware; reduction fired, cone 10;
multiple glaze layers over shino base glaze
PHOTO BY ARTIST

Mark Peters

Untitled, 2003

8 x 9 x 7 inches (20.3 x 22.9 x 17.8 cm)
Wheel-thrown and altered stoneware;
cone 10; salt glaze
PHOTO BY ARTIST

Tyler Gulden

Pitcher with Covered Spout, 1998

9 x 4 x 6 inches (22.9 x 10.2 x 15.2 cm)
Wheel-thrown porcelain; anagama
fired, cone 12
PHOTO BY ARTIST

Claudia Dunaway

Milk Pitcher, 2004

6 x 6 x 5½ inches (15.2 x 15.2 x 14 cm)
Wheel-thrown and altered white stoneware;
gas fired in reduction,
cone 10; color slips and wax line detail
PHOTO BY TOM MILLS

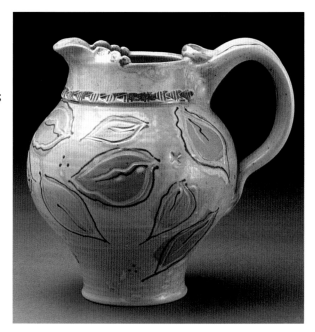

Lynn Smiser Bowers

Pitcher with Striped Spout, 2004

7 x 7 x 5 inches (17.8 x 17.8 x 12.7 cm)
Wheel-thrown porcelain; gas fired in reduction,
cone 10; wax resist and oxide details
PHOTO BY E.G. SCHEMPF

Annie Singletary

| *Square Pitcher*, 2004

24 x 6 x 6 inches (61 x 15.2 x 15.2 cm)
Porcelain; reduction fired, cone 10
PHOTO BY STEVE MANN

Kate Shakeshaft Murray

Tiger Fur Pitcher, 2005

10 x 7 x 5 inches (25.4 x 17.8 x 12.7 cm)
Wheel-thrown porcelain; gas fired in reduction,
cone 10; glazes layered with wax resist
PHOTO BY ARTIST

Sandi Pierantozzi

Creamers, 2005

5 x 4 x 3 inches each (12.7 x 10.2 x 7.6 cm)
Slab-built porcelain; electric fired, cone 6
PHOTO BY ARTIST

Gillian J. Parke

| *Three-Legged Shino Pitcher*, 2005

9¾ x 5 x 5 inches (24.8 x 12.7 x 12.7 cm)
Wheel-thrown porcelain; gas fired, cone 10;
shino glaze and feldspar inclusion
PHOTO BY SETH TICE-LEWIS

Nick Ramey

Untitled, 2005

9 x 6 x 5 inches (22.9 x 15.2 x 12.7 cm)
Wheel-thrown and altered stoneware; wood
fired with soda, cone 11; black underglaze
PHOTO BY ARTIST

Mark Peters

Untitled, 2002

11 x 7 x 6 inches (27.9 x 17.8 x 15.2 cm)
Wheel-thrown stoneware; wood fired,
cone 10; applied and natural ash, shino
and black glazes
PHOTO BY ARTIST

The process of heat and time are baked into Mark Peters' pot. The glazes softened and ran into one another in beautiful, unpredictable ways. This kind of collaboration between potter and fire is one of the alluring characteristics of atmospheric kilns. —TG

Marilyn Dennis Palsha

Green Sauce Pitcher, 2002

7 x 5½ x 3 inches (17.8 x 14 x 7.6 cm)
Slab-built earthenware; electric fired,
cone 02; majolica
PHOTO BY SETH TICE-LEWIS

Karl Knudson

Pitcher, 2004

9 x 7 x 3 inches (22.9 x 17.8 x 7.6 cm)
Wheel-thrown stoneware; reduction
fired, cone 10; multiple matte and
wood ash glazes
PHOTO BY BILL BACHUBER

Hwang Jeng-daw

Metal Pitcher, 2004

6¼ x 6¾ x 4¼ inches (16 x 17 x 11 cm)
Wheel-thrown stoneware; gas fired in
reduction, cone 9; luster, cone 0/3
PHOTO BY FUN UEE

Peter Pilven

Wood-Fired Pitcher I, 2003

8¼ x 4¼ inches (21 x 11 cm)
Hand-built stoneware; anagama
fired; reactive slips
PHOTO BY ARTIST

Lis Ehrenreich

Pitcher with Beak, 2004

10½ x 3½ inches (26.5 x 9 cm)
Wheel-thrown Danish red earthenware;
electric fired in reduction, 2138°F
(1170°C); engobe, ash glaze
PHOTOS BY ERIK BALLE POVLSEN

Michael Organ

Harvest Jug, 2003

16 x 18 x 13 inches (40.6 x 45.7 x 33 cm)
Coil-built terra cotta; oxidation fired, cone 04;
trailed slip, relief decoration, transparent glaze
PHOTO BY FFOTOGRAFF PHOTO LIBRARY AND AGENCY

Michael Organ has created his piece as if it were some precious
gem-encrusted object of the Medieval Court. There is a playful
sense of risk and abandon in the opulent surface treatment. —*TG*

Rachel L. Delk

Pumpkin Pitcher, 2005

4 x 6½ x 4 inches (10.2 x 16.5 x 10.2 cm)
Wheel-thrown and altered; cone 6
PHOTO BY RICHARD NICKEL AND ARTIST

Emily Murphy

Crosshatched Oval Pitcher, 2005

9 x 3½ x 6 inches (22.9 x 8.9 x 15.2 cm)
Wheel-thrown and altered stoneware;
reduction fired, cone 10; layered slips
PHOTOS BY GUY NICOL

Becca Floyd

Untitled, 2005

6½ x 2½ x 6 inches (16.5 x 6.4 x 15.2 cm)
Stoneware; reduction fired, cone 10; shino
and yellow washes
PHOTO BY MICHAEL DAVIE

Daniel Brown

Wood-Fired Pitcher, 2004

17 x 10 x 11 inches
(43.2 x 25.4 x 27.9 cm)
Stoneware; wood fired; feldspathic
inclusions, natural ash glaze
PHOTO BY ARTIST

Christian Kuharik

Ash-Glazed Pitcher, 2004

10½ x 6 x 6 inches (26.7 x 15.2 x 15.2 cm)
Wheel-thrown porcelain; reduction
fired, cone 10
PHOTO BY ARTIST

Pang Swee Tuan

Coral, 2005

9½ x 7½ x 6¼ inches
(24 x 19 x 16 cm)
Wheel-thrown; electric
fired, cone 6; double-walled
construction; pierced decoration
PHOTOS BY CHAN HON ONN

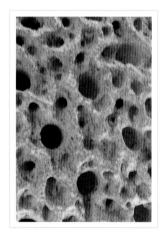

Bayard Morgan

| Untitled, 2004

11 x 5 x 6 inches
(27.9 x 12.7 x 15.2 cm)
Wheel-thrown stoneware;
wood fired, cone 10
PHOTO BY PETER LEE

Joe J. Singewald

│ *Shino Pitcher,* 2003

8 x 5 x 5 inches (20.3 x 12.7 x 12.7 cm)
Stoneware; wood fired in reduction, cone 10
PHOTO BY PETER LEE

Emily Reason

│ *Lidded Pitcher,* 2005

8 x 6 x 5 inches (20.3 x 15.2 x 12.7 cm)
Wheel-thrown porcelain; reduction
fired, cone 10
PHOTO BY ARTIST

Janet Murie

Untitled, 2002

15 x 8 inches (38.1 x 20.3 cm)
Wheel-thrown stoneware; gas
fired, cone 11; ash glaze over
rutile blue glaze

PHOTO BY MEL MITTERMILLER

Roberta Shapiro

In the Garden, 2004

8 x 6 x 4 inches (20.3 x 15.2 x 10.2 cm)
Wheel-thrown porcelain, hand-built
handle; gas fired, cone 10; stains,
underglazes, clear glaze
PHOTO BY JOE GIUNTA

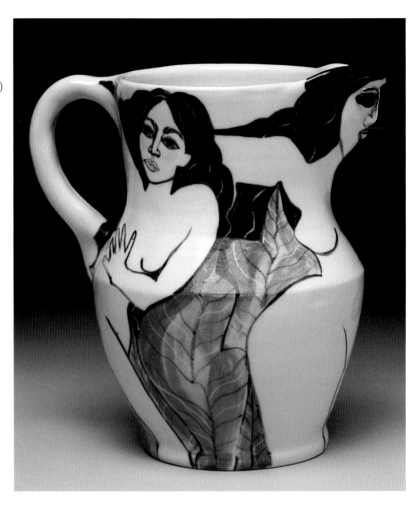

On my vessels, female forms undulate with floral themes,
marrying form and surface decoration. —RS

Vukicevic Velimir

Never Enough, 2001

11¾ x 11¾ x 15¾ inches
(30 x 30 x 40 cm)
Wheel-thrown porcelain;
electric fired, cone 10; slip
and glaze decoration
PHOTO BY VLADIMIR POPOVIC

Bruce Gholson

Untitled, 2004

14 x 6 x 6 inches each (35.6 x 15.2 x 15.2 cm)
Thrown porcelain; electric fired, cone 7–8
PHOTO BY ARTIST

North Carolina enjoys a rich pottery tradition; both old-time and contemporary approaches are thriving today. Bruce Gholson presents his version of a famous Carolina North State–style form, the biblically referenced "Rebecca pitcher." —*TG*

Diane Rosenmiller

Untitled, 2004

8 x 7 x 5 inches (20.3 x 17.8 x 12.7 cm)
Wheel-thrown and altered porcelain;
soda fired, cone 10

PHOTO BY NICHOLAS SEIDNER

John Kudlacek

Ring Pitcher, 1995

10½ x 9½ x 1½ inches
(26.7 x 24.1 x 3.8 cm)
Wheel-thrown stoneware;
reduction fired, cone 10
PHOTOS BY ARTIST

Although abstracted from the functional pitcher, this piece contains
all of the parts. One end presents the handle, the opposite the
spout, and the remainder the container. —JK

Lesley Baker

Untitled, 2000

12 x 12 x 5 inches (30.5 x 30.5 x 12.7 cm)
Slip cast and assembled porcelain; gas fired
in reduction, cone 6
PHOTO BY ARTIST

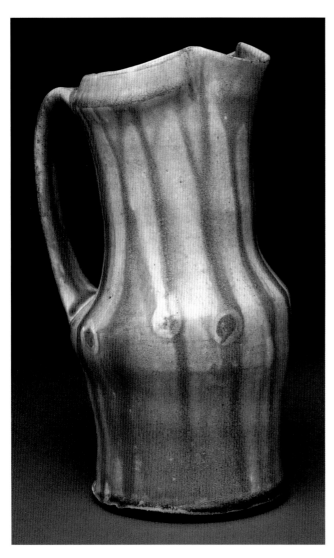

Josh Copus

Water Inspired Pitcher, 2004

10 x 5 x 4 inches (25.4 x 12.7 x 10.2 cm)
Wheel-thrown stoneware; wood fired,
cone 11; ash glaze
PHOTO BY ARTIST

Cynthia Bringle

Soda-Fired Pitcher, 2005

9 x 9 x 8 inches (22.9 x 22.9 x 20.3 cm)
Wheel-thrown, cut, and faceted porcelain;
soda fired, cone 10; slip decoration
PHOTO BY TOM MILLS

Bradley C. Birkhimer

Untitled, 2005

9½ x 7 x 7 inches (24.1 x 17.8 x 17.8 cm)
Wheel-thrown porcelain; wood fired with soda,
cone 11; ash with cobalt and Nuka ash glazes
PHOTO BY ARTIST

Jared Ward

Pitcher with Cup Storage, 2004

Assembled: 10 x 6 x 5 inches
(25.4 x 15.2 x 12.7 cm)
Wheel-thrown and extruded stoneware
and porcelain; reduction fired, cone 10;
oxidation fired, cone 9; sprayed glazes
PHOTO BY ARTIST

I am interested in creating ceramic vessels that function as containers for other
ceramic vessels, or objects that carry or protect smaller objects. Pieces are concealed
on the interior of a large vessel and then, when removed, are essential to the
function of the piece as a whole. This family of pieces works as a community to
create something greater than any of its individual parts. —JW

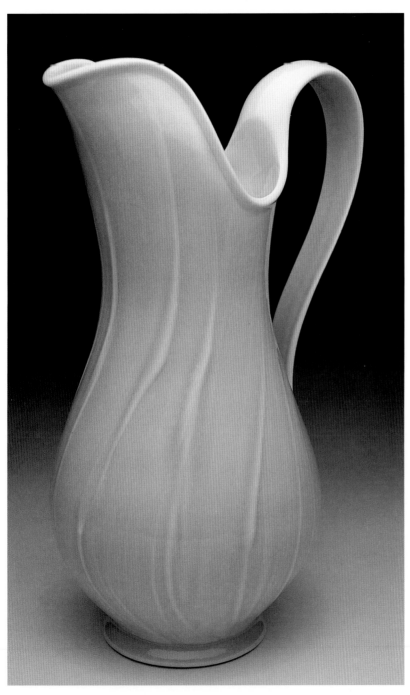

Monica Ripley

Water Pitcher, 2004

12 x 7 x 4 inches (30.5 x 17.8 x 10.2 cm)
Wheel-thrown and altered porcelain; gas
fired in oxidation, cone 10; slip decoration
PHOTO BY ARTIST

Jeanette Rakowski

Untitled, 2002

14 x 7 x 7 inches (35.6 x 17.8 x 17.8 cm)
Wheel-thrown stoneware; soda fired, cone 10
PHOTO BY JOSH DEWEESE

Jennifer Everett

Pitcher and Tumblers, 2003

Pitcher: 7½ x 6 x 6 inches (19 x 15.2 x 15.2 cm);
Tumblers: 5 x 3 x 3 inches each (12.7 x 7.6 x 7.6 cm)
Wheel-thrown stoneware; reduction fired, cone 10;
stamped and carved decoration; glazes with wax resist
PHOTO BY ARTIST

Char Anderson
Larry Anderson

Holey Cow, 2004

5 x 5 x 4 inches
(12.7 x 12.7 x 10.2 cm)
Wheel-thrown and altered
porcelain; electric fired,
cone 10; crystalline glaze
PHOTO BY WARREN SMITH

Char and Larry Anderson present their accomplished skill with crystalline glaze. They have wisely chosen a simple yet sophisticated form as a subtle vehicle to carry an arrestingly beautiful surface. —*TG*

Geoffrey Swindell

Cream Jug, 2004

4¾ x 2¼ x 3 inches (12 x 6 x 7.5 cm)
Wheel-thrown porcelain; oxidation fired,
cone 8; copper and vanadium glazes
PHOTO BY ARTIST

Randy Carlson

| *Pitcher with Iron and Rutile Stain,* 2004

7½ x 6 x 3 inches (19 x 15.2 x 7.6 cm)
Wheel-thrown and altered stoneware;
reduction fired, cone 10
PHOTO BY DUANE ZEHR

Scott Dooley

| *Zigzag Watering Can,* 2003

15 x 12 x 5 inches (38.1 x 30.5 x 12.7 cm)
Slab-built porcelain; electric fired, cone 5
PHOTO BY ARTIST

Lilach Lotan

Untitled, 2004

19 x 8½ x 5½ inches (48.3 x 21.6 x 14 cm)
Wheel-thrown and altered stoneware;
wood fired in anagama kiln, cone 12
PHOTOS BY RON LOTAN

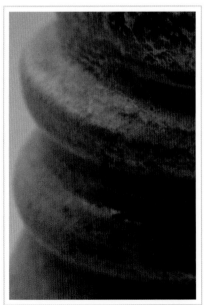

Joy Tanner

Creamer, 2004

5½ x 6 x 4½ inches (14 x 15.2 x 11.4 cm)
Wheel-thrown and altered porcelaneous
stoneware; salt and soda fired, cone 10;
combed incision through slip
PHOTO BY ARTIST

Conner McKissack

Pitcher, 2004

8 x 10 x 6 inches
(20.3 x 25.4 x 15.2 cm)
Wheel-thrown porcelain;
soda fired, cone 10
PHOTO BY ARTIST

Ben Jensen

Pitcher with Waves, 2005

9 x 9 x 8 inches (22.9 x 22.9 x 20.3 cm)
Wheel-thrown porcelain; salt fired,
reduction cooled, cone 11
PHOTO BY DAN OJEDA

David Pier

Pitcher, Style #2, 2003

7 x 8 x 9½ inches
(17.8 x 20.3 x 24.1 cm)
Slip-cast porcelain; oxidation
fired, cone 10
PHOTO BY ARTIST

We have all experienced pitchers that are clumsy to use—they do not pour well or are hard to hold. Making things that work well for people is a big challenge studio potters share with product designers and architects. There are many creative solutions to the problem, and I appreciate pots like David Pier's that test these parameters in the search for individual solutions. —*TG*

Shelley Schreiber

Sage Pitcher, 2005

12½ x 8 x 5 inches (31.8 x 20.3 x 12.7 cm)
Wheel-thrown and hand-built porcelain;
reduction fired, cone 10; hand-carved
bas relief

PHOTO BY ARTIST

Karla Ricker

Pitcher Jug, 2004

12 x 7 x 8 inches
(30.5 x 17.8 x 20.3 cm)
Wheel-thrown and hand-built
stoneware; wood fired in
anagama kiln, cone 10
PHOTO BY ARTIST

Sally Campbell

Little Bear Pitcher, 2004

8 x 8 x 7 inches (20.3 x 20.3 x 17.8 cm)
Wheel-thrown and altered porcelain;
soda fired, cone 11
PHOTOS BY ARTIST

Brian J. Taylor

Untitled, 2003

6 x 5 x 8 inches (15.2 x 12.7 x 20.3 cm)
Stoneware; soda fired, cone 10; slips, glazes
PHOTO BY ARTIST

Ken Turner

Untitled, 2003

8 x 8 x 6 inches
(20.3 x 20.3 x 15.2 cm)
Wheel-thrown and altered
porcelain; gas fired in
reduction, cone 10
PHOTO BY TOM HOLT

Rene Barkett

Minneapolis, 2003

17 x 7 x 6 inches (43.2 x 17.8 x 15.2 cm)
Wheel-thrown and altered porcelain;
electric fired, cone 6
PHOTO BY D. JAMES DEE

Rosalie Wynkoop

Majolica Pitcher, 2003

4 x 3¾ x 2¾ inches (10.2 x 9.5 x 7 cm)
Wheel-thrown terra cotta; electric fired, cone
03; tin glaze; luster, china paint, cone 018
PHOTO BY JOSH DEWEESE

Lucy Fagella

Creamer, 2004

4½ x 4 x 3 inches (11.4 x 10.2 x 7.6 cm)
Wheel-thrown, altered, and stamped
porcelain; electric fired, cone 6
PHOTO BY JOHN POLAK

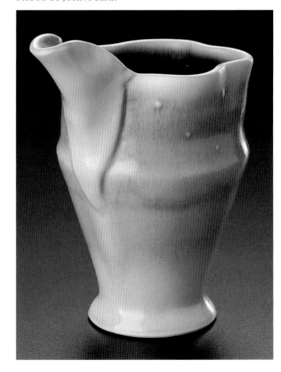

Amy Evans

Untitled, 2004

12 x 5 x 5 inches (30.5 x 12.7 x 12.7 cm)
Wheel-thrown stoneware; soda fired, cone 9
PHOTO BY CHUCK MCMAHON AND ARTIST

Chris Longwell

DeCanter, 2005

8 x 5 x 4 inches (20.3 x 12.7 x 10.2 cm)
Wheel-thrown porcelain; soda fired,
cone 10; slips and glazes
PHOTO BY ARTIST

David Grainger
Kelli Sinner

Don Quixote Pitcher, 2004

11 x 7 x 5 inches (27.9 x 17.8 x 12.7 cm)
Wheel-thrown porcelain; gas fired,
cone 10; underglaze
PHOTO BY D. JAMES DEE

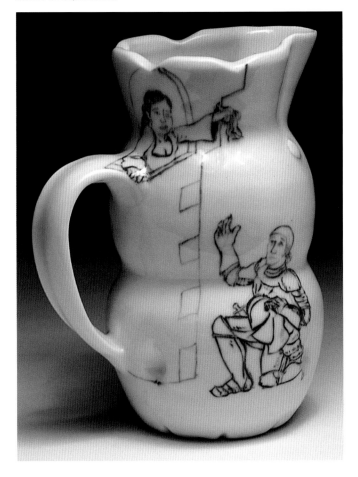

Sara Patterson

Pitcher with Double Handle, 2001

8 x 6 x 6 inches (20.3 x 15.2 x 15.2 cm)
Wheel-thrown stoneware; wood fired,
cone 10; wax resist decoration
PHOTOS BY D. JAMES DEE

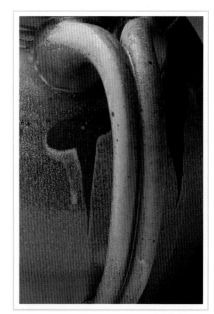

It's the details that give a pot its merit and personality. It reflects each potter's touch and personal approach to clay, such as the handle that Sara Patterson fashioned for her pitcher. —TG

Ryan Forrey

Shino Pitcher, 2005

8 x 6 x 5 inches
(20.3 x 15.2 x 12.7 cm)
Wheel-thrown porcelain;
reduction fired with soda, cone 10
PHOTO BY ARTIST

Patti Hughes

| Untitled, 2004

5¾ x 4¾ x 3¾ inches (14.6 x 12 x 9.5 cm)
Wheel-thrown and altered stoneware;
reduction fired, cone 10; celadon glaze
PHOTO BY TIM BARKLEY

Dick Cunningham

| *Red and Blue Pitcher*, 2005

4 x 5½ x 3¾ inches (10.2 x 14 x 9.5 cm)
Wheel-thrown stoneware; electric fired, cone 6
PHOTO BY JOHN WOODEN

Shawn Ireland

Pitcher, 2004

10 inches tall (25.4 cm)
Stoneware and local clay; wood fired,
cones 9 to 10; ash glaze
PHOTO BY WALKER MONTGOMERY

Rosalie Wynkoop

| *Majolica Pitcher,* 2003

4 x 3¾ x 2¾ inches (10.2 x 9.5 x 7 cm)
Wheel-thrown terra cotta; electric fired, cone
03; tin glaze; luster, china paint, cone 018
PHOTO BY JOSH DEWEESE

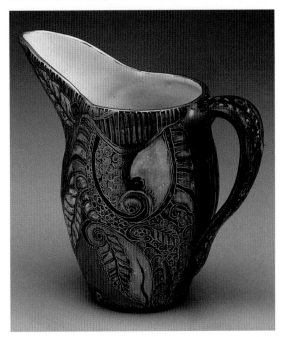

Joy Tanner

| *Leaf-Carved Pitcher,* 2005

7 x 7½ x 6 inches (17.8 x 19 x 15.2 cm)
Wheel-thrown and carved porcelain; salt
and soda fired, cone 10; sprayed slip
PHOTO BY ARTIST

Sangria Pitcher, 2004

16 x 8 x 3½ inches (40.6 x 20.3 x 8.9 cm)
Wheel-thrown, altered, and stacked
stoneware; cone 10; salt glaze
PHOTO BY TOM MILLS

Colin Johnson

Untitled, 2001

7¾ x 5 inches (19.7 x 12.7 cm)
Wheel-thrown earthenware with pulled
handle and roulette decoration; electric
fired, cone 5; tin glaze
PHOTO BY ARTIST

Genna Grushovenko

Soda Pitcher, 2004

12 x 8 x 8 inches (30.5 x 20.3 x 20.3 cm)
Wheel-thrown stoneware; gas and soda
fired, cone 10; glazes
PHOTO BY ARTIST

Susan A. Beecher

Dragonfly Pitcher, 2003

10 x 7 x 5 inches (25.4 x 17.8 x 12.7 cm)
Wheel-thrown white stoneware; wood fired,
cone 10; salt glaze and slip
PHOTO BY D. JAMES DEE

Jody Johnstone

Untitled, 2004

10½ x 5 inches (26.7 x 12.7 cm)
Stoneware; anagama fired, cone 10
PHOTO BY DAVID ORSER

Elizabeth Kendall

Untitled, 2005

3 x 3 x 2 inches (7.6 x 7.6 x 5 cm)
Slab-built porcelain; gas fired in
Minnesota flat-top car kiln, cone 10;
Oribe variation with .5% cobalt
oxide added; rim dipped in glass frit
PHOTO BY ARTIST

A pitcher is not really a container but a dispenser. It has an active
and giving role on the table. What's poured into it is intended to
pour out. Hand building with soft slabs allows me to echo this
activity in the undulations of the form. —EK

Mark Rossier

Blakley Buttermilk Jug, 2005

9 x 7 x 7 inches (22.9 x 17.8 x 17.8 cm)
Wheel-thrown stoneware; gas fired, cone
6; slip-trailed decoration
PHOTO BY ARTIST

Judy Vasseur

Small Pitchers, 2004

Left: 4½ x 3¼ x 4 inches (11.4 x 8.3 x 10.2 cm);
Right: 4½ x 3½ x 4¾ inches (11.4 x 8.9 x 12 cm)
Wheel-thrown stoneware; reduction fired, cone 10
PHOTO BY D. JAMES DEE

Hank Goodman

Untitled, 2003

12 x 6 x 6 inches (30.5 x 15.2 x 15.2 cm)
Wheel-thrown and altered stoneware; gas
fired in reduction, cone 10; shino glaze
PHOTO BY TIM BARNWELL

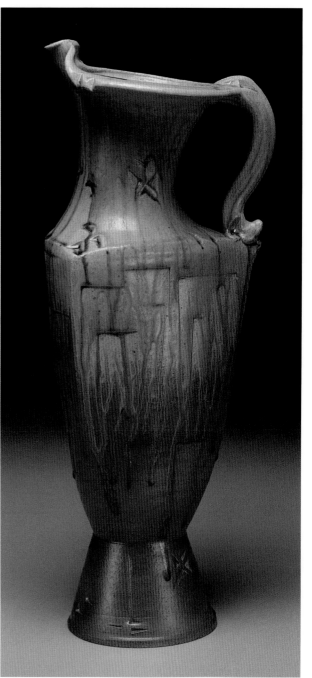

Kate Fisher

| *Pitcher,* 2004

11 x 4½ x 4½ inches (27.9 x 11.4 x 11.4 cm)
Wheel-thrown and altered porcelain; oxidation
fired, cone 6; porcelain slip
PHOTO BY MARK BUTLER

Laurel MacDuffie

| *Small Pitcher with Tray,* 2004

Overall: 5 x 4 x 3 inches (12.7 x 10.2 x 7.6 cm)
Wheel-thrown local clay; cone 10;
salt and ash glaze
PHOTO BY ARTIST

Nicholas Bernard

Blue Ewer, 2005

17 x 10 x 10 inches
(43.2 x 25.4 x 25.4 cm)
Wheel-thrown, altered, and
coil-built earthenware;
multi-fired in oxidation,
cone 03; layers of colored
slips and oxides
PHOTO BY ARTIST

Dawn Oakford

Fragments, 1995

10½ x 10½ x 4¾ inches (27 x 27 x 12 cm)
Slip-cast stoneware; electric fired; underglaze colors
and clear glaze, 2300°F (1260°C)
PHOTO BY JOHN FARROW

Daniel Gegen

Bird-Beaked Pitcher, 2004

12 x 9 x 7 inches (30.5 x 22.9 x 17.8 cm)
Wheel-thrown and assembled terra cotta;
electric fired, cone 03; slips and glazes
PHOTO BY ARTIST

David C. Harder

Old-World Tuscany Pitcher, 2005

15 x 8 x 9½ inches (38.1 x 20.3 x 24.1 cm)
Wheel-thrown white stoneware; reduction
fired, cone 10; high-fire glaze
PHOTO BY ARTIST

Bonnie Staffel

Through the Gorge, 2003

23 x 11 x 11 inches (58.4 x 27.9 x 27.9 cm)
Coil-built and thrown stoneware; bisque
fired, cone 08; pit fired with copper
PHOTO BY STEVE KOSTYSHYN

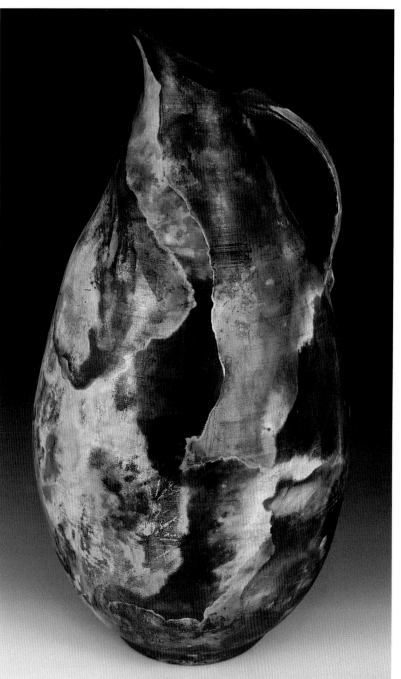

Bruce Gholson

Untitled, 2004

8½ x 10 x 6½ inches (21.6 x 25.4 x 16.5 cm)
Wheel-thrown, altered, and assembled porcelain; electric
fired, cone 7/8
PHOTO BY ARTIST

Virginia Mitford-Taylor

Cobalt Blue Pitcher, 2005

6½ x 2½ x 7½ inches (16.5 x 6.4 x 19 cm)
Wheel-thrown and altered stoneware; gas
fired in reduction, cone 10; sprayed white
glaze over cobalt blue glaze
PHOTO BY PATRICK CRABB

Toby Rosenberg

Calla Lily Pint Pitcher, 2004

8¼ x 4 inches (21 x 10.2 cm)
White stoneware with slab-built, embossed
design and coil handle; electric fired,
cone 7; glaze on glaze and copper sulfate
colorants; 24-karat gold, cone 019
PHOTO BY MICHAEL BARRIAULT

The embossed calla lily
pattern comes from an
antique cut-linen bureau
scarf. I let the edge of the
cutwork inform the lip of
the pitcher. —*TR*

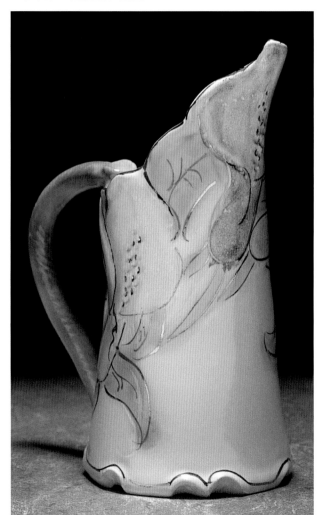

Farraday Newsome

Promise of the Garden, 2001

18 x 18 x 14 inches (45.7 x 45.7 x 35.6 cm)
Wheel-thrown terra cotta; electric fired, cone 05
PHOTO BY ARTIST

Inspired by tropical fruit, Farraday Newsome has created an opulent pitcher that would be most welcomed filled with cold, refreshing drinks at a lively summer gathering. —*TG*

Pitcher, 2004

12 x 7 x 6 inches (30.5 x 17.8 x 15.2 cm)
Porcelain; wood fired, cone 10
PHOTO BY ARTIST

Heather Newman

Wood-Fired Pitcher, 2005

10 x 6½ x 6 inches (25.4 x 16.5 x 15.2 cm)
Stoneware; wood fired, cone 12
PHOTO BY STEVE MANN

Matt Nolen

Resistance/Adaptation, 2004

29 x 12 x 8 inches (73.7 x 30.5 x 20.3 cm)
Wheel-thrown and altered white stoneware;
multiple electric firings, cone 6; glaze, cone 04;
china paint, luster, and photo decals, cone 018
PHOTO BY D. JAMES DEE

I explore the metaphor of
landscape and the role that
water plays in the creation
and dissolution of the life
cycle: vapor and dust. Man's
evolution from dry desert or
lush, fertile landscapes—and
the worldviews that develop
in relationship to each
extreme environment—
inform the pitchers, basins,
and fountains that compose
this body of work. —*MN*

Janna Ferris

Fruit and Vegetable Pitcher, 2001

21½ x 9 inches (55 x 23 cm)
Wheel-thrown earthenware; oxidation fired,
2156°F (1180°C); sprig additions, underglazes,
transparent glaze
PHOTO BY IAN HOBBS

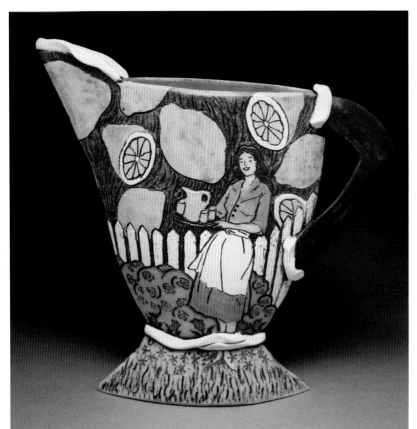

Jennifer Mettlen Nolan

Gren-Aid, 2005

12 x 9 x 4 inches (30.5 x 22.9 x 10.2 cm)
Slab-built and carved stoneware; cone 04;
velvet underglazes, low-fire stains
PHOTOS BY SHELDON GANSTROM

Jennifer Mettlen Nolan
sets up an eccentric dichot-
omy between images on
opposite sides of this
pitcher, tied together by
her pun-like title. —*TG*

Elaine Pinkernell

Big Bird Pitcher, 2003

15 x 13 x 4 inches (38.1 x 33 x 10.2 cm)
Slab-built stoneware; gas fired, cone 10;
soft-clay construction
PHOTO BY GEORGE POST

Lynn Fisher

Poinsettia Pitcher, 2005

3 x 6 x 3 inches (7.6 x 15.2 x 7.6 cm)
Hand-built porcelain; electric fired,
cone 9; impressed and joined leaf slabs
PHOTO BY STEVE KOSTYSHYN

Bonnie Seeman

Untitled, 2005

5 x 7½ x 6 inches
(12.7 x 19 x 15.2 cm)
Wheel-thrown and hand-built
porcelain; electric fired, cone 10
PHOTO BY ARTIST
COURTESY OF GALLERY OMR,
MEXICO CITY, MEXICO

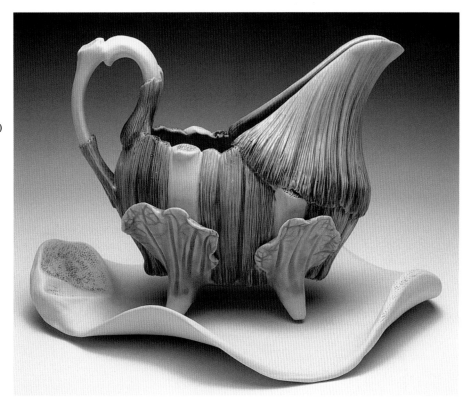

Nature has long offered inspiration to potters; perhaps the earliest model for pitchers
were cupped leaves and hollowed vegetables. Bonnie Seeman and Lynn Fisher offer
two interpretations of sauceboats seemingly contrived from leaves. —*TG*

Rosalie Wynkoop

Majolica Pitcher, 2004

4½ x 4 x 3 (11.4 x 10.2 x 7.6 cm)
Wheel-thrown terra cotta; electric fired, cone
03; tin glaze; luster, china paint, cone 018
PHOTO BY JOSH DEWEESE

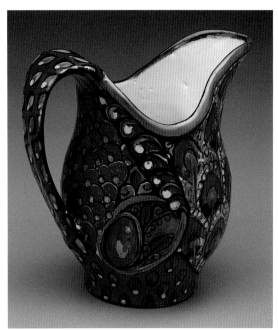

Jillian Higley

Untitled, 2002

6 x 7 x 6 inches (15.2 x 17.8 x 15.2 cm)
Altered, carved, and thrown white
stoneware; fired, cone 5
PHOTO BY BART KASTEN

Patrick L. Dougherty

Bad Moon Rising, 1988

18 x 7¾ inches (45.7 x 19.7 cm)
Wheel-thrown earthenware; electric
fired in oxidation, cone 04; painted
with underglazes, clear glaze
PHOTO BY JAY BACHEMIN

Patrick L. Dougherty
exploits the bright,
crisp colors available
at earthenware
firing temperatures,
enveloping this pitcher
in swirling, fantastic
figural imagery. —*TG*

J. Daniel Murphy

| *Wood-Fired Pitcher*, 2005

12 x 5 x 6 inches (30.5 x 12.7 x 15.2 cm)
Wheel-thrown iron-rich clay; wood fired,
cone 8; bone ash glaze
PHOTO BY ARTIST

Monica Ripley

| *Creamer*, 2004

4½ x 6 x 4 inches (11.4 x 15.2 x 10.2 cm)
Wheel-thrown and altered porcelain; gas
fired in oxidation, cone 10; slip decoration
PHOTO BY ARTIST

Suze Lindsay

Sangria Pitcher, 2001

16 x 8¼ x 4 inches (40.6 x 21 x 10.2 cm)
Wheel-thrown, altered, and stacked
stoneware; cone 10; salt glaze
PHOTO BY TOM MILLS

Becca Floyd

Untitled, 2005

6½ x 2½ x 6 inches (16.5 x 6.4 x 15.2 cm)
Stoneware; gas fired in reduction, cone 10;
shino and Oribe glazes
PHOTO BY MICHAEL DAVIE

Liz Smith

| *Pitcher*, 2005

9 x 7 x 5 inches (22.9 x 17.8 x 12.7 cm)
Thrown, altered, press molded, and
carved porcelain; electric fired, cone 06;
decals, cone 019
PHOTO BY ARTIST

Liz Smith appears to have pieced together floral decals and cast details of
Victorian-era table settings. She maintains the precious qualities of that
earlier ware in this elegant piece. —*TG*

Neil Estrick

Untitled, 2005

10 x 5 x 5 inches (25.4 x 12.7 x 12.7 cm)
Wheel-thrown porcelain; reduction fired, cone 10
PHOTO BY ARTIST

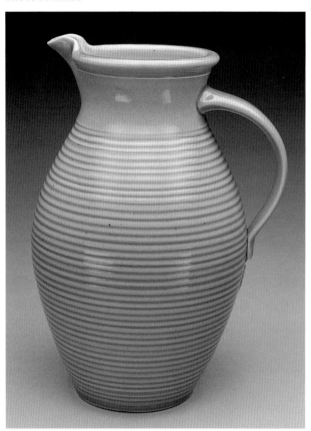

Chris Gray

Four Crows Pitcher, 2005

6 x 4 x 5½ inches (15.2 x 10.2 x 14 cm)
Wheel-thrown and stamped porcelain;
electric fired, cone 10
PHOTO BY ARTIST

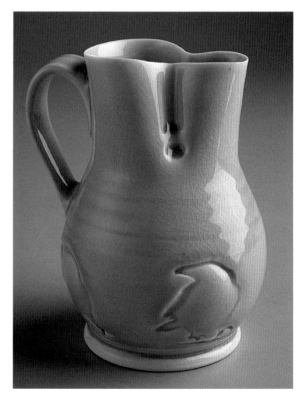

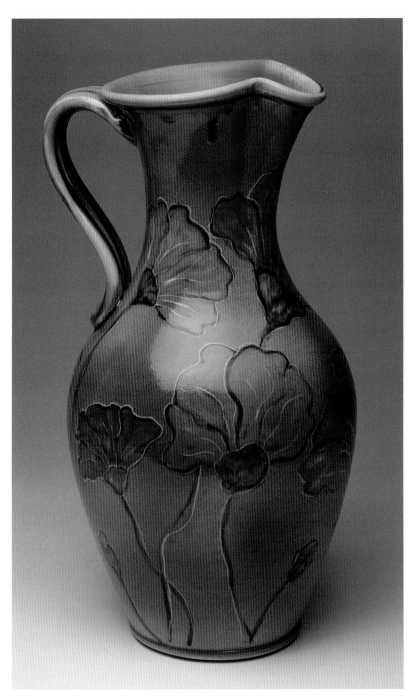

Cindy Eve

Poppy Pitcher, 2004

17½ x 10½ x 9½ inches
(44.5 x 26.7 x 24.1 cm)
Wheel-thrown porcelain;
electric fired, cone 6
PHOTO BY MCMILLAN STUDIO

Kristen Kieffer

Creamer, 2005

5 x 5 x 3½ inches (12.7 x 12.7 x 8.9 cm)
Wheel-thrown and altered white
stoneware; soda fired, cone 10;
slip trail and carved decoration
PHOTO BY ARTIST

Kristen Kieffer gives particular attention to detail. The lip is especially sensitive,
with a nuanced spout and subtle cutouts on both sides of the body. —*TG*

Beth Stofleth

| *Pitcher*, 2004

7 inches tall (17.8 cm)
Wheel-thrown stoneware;
wood fired with soda, cone 10
PHOTO BY JEFF BRUCE

Nicholas Seidner

Pitcher, 2003

11 x 6 x 6 inches (27.9 x 15.2 x 15.2 cm)
Wheel-thrown and altered stoneware; gas
fired with salt and soda, cone 10
PHOTO BY ARTIST

Gloria Singer

Untitled, 2005

6 x 6 x 4 inches (15.2 x 15.2 x 10.2 cm)
Wheel-thrown stoneware; electric fired,
cone 6½; fake ash glazes
PHOTO BY ARTIST

Brad Tucker

Untitled, 2005

14 x 9 inches (35.6 x 22.9 cm)
Wheel-thrown stoneware; gas fired
in reduction, cone 10; ash glazes
PHOTO BY SETH TICE-LEWIS

Steven Hill

Pitcher, 2004

12 x 9 x 8 inches (30.5 x 22.9 x 20.3 cm)
Wheel-thrown and altered stoneware; single
fired, cone 10; ribbed slip design, multiple
sprayed glazes
PHOTO BY AL SURRATT

Stephen Driver

| *Paddled Pitcher*, 2003

7 x 4 inches (17.8 x 10.2 cm)
Wheel-thrown, paddled, and cut
stoneware; wood fired in anagama kiln
PHOTO BY GEORGE CHAMBERS

Forrest Lesch-Middelton

| *Wood-Fired Pitcher*, 2004

10 x 7 inches (25.4 x 17.8 cm)
Wheel-thrown stoneware; wood
fired, cone 10
PHOTO BY ARTIST

Peter Knuckey

Wine Carafe, 1989

11¾ x 5 x 10½ inches (30 x 12.5 x 26.5 cm)
Wheel-thrown stoneware; wood fired in reduction,
cone 10; salt glaze
PHOTO BY ARTIST

Heather O'Brien

Tako Soy Bottle, 2001

5 x 2 x 2 inches (12.7 x 5 x 5 cm)
Pinched, coiled, and thrown
stoneware; electric fired, cone 6
PHOTO BY LUIS GARCIA

Lesley Baker

French Curve, 2001

14 x 6 x 5 inches (35.6 x 15.2 x 12.7 cm)
Slip cast and assembled porcelain; gas fired
in reduction, cone 6
PHOTO BY ARTIST

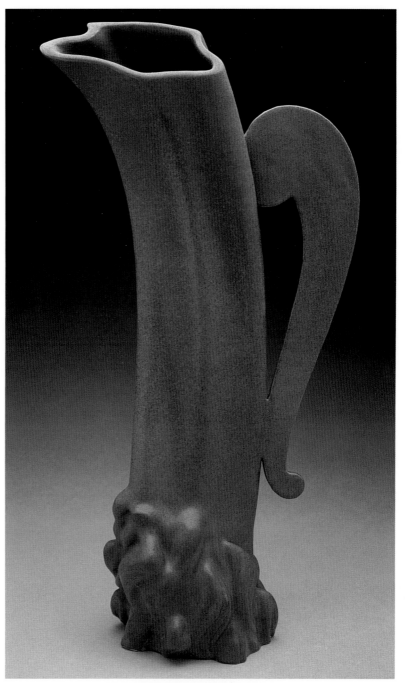

Wes Harvey

Striped Pitcher, 2005

10 x 6 x 4 inches (25.4 x 15.2 x 10.2 cm)
Slip-cast porcelain; electric fired, cone 04;
decals, cone 020

PHOTO BY ARTIST

Brad McLemore

Yellow Pitcher, 2005

11½ x 6½ x 5½ inches (29.2 x 16.5 x 14 cm)
Wheel-thrown porcelain; reduction fired
with soda, cone 10
PHOTO BY ARTIST

Brad McLemore has
created a pitcher
that defies a snap
judgment. The
quirky division of the
cylindrical form into
three segments
suggests that he's
experimenting with
the parameters of
what is expected,
perhaps exploring
other wheel-based
ways to make
a pitcher. —*TG*

Patrick Coughlin

Fifty-Gallon Drum Gravy Boat, 2005

11 x 9 x 5 inches (27.9 x 22.9 x 12.7 cm)
Hand-built earthenware; cone 04; terra
sigillatta, low-fire washes
PHOTO BY ARTIST

Ian F. Thomas

Pitcher, 2005

6 x 4¾ x 5½ inches (15.2 x 12.1 x 14 cm)
Wheel-thrown and altered white stoneware;
reduction fired with salt and soda, cone 10
PHOTO BY ARTIST

Lynnette Ratzlaff

Untitled, 2005

7¼ x 7½ x 7 inches (18.4 x 19 x 17.8 cm)
Stoneware; gas fired, cone 5; glaze, overglaze
PHOTO BY NICOLE COPEL

McKenzie Smith

Untitled, 2002

12 x 7 x 7 inches (30.5 x 17.8 x 17.8 cm)
Thrown stoneware; salt and soda
fired, cone 10

PHOTO BY ARTIST

Trent Burkett

| Untitled, 2004

11 x 8 x 7 inches (27.9 x 20.3 x 17.8 cm)
Wheel-thrown porcelain; wood
fired, cone 12
PHOTO BY ARTIST

There can be great power in the marks that potters make on pots. Trent Burkett
offers a simple, almost accidental mark on the upper belly of his pitcher, while
McKenzie Smith painted a gestural floral image against an understated surface. —TG

Clarice Ann Dorst

Green Pitcher, 2005

9½ x 8 x 6 inches (24.1 x 20.3 x 15.2 cm)
Wheel-thrown stoneware; gas fired in
reduction, cone 10
PHOTO BY ARTIST

Elise Hauenstein

Pitcher, 2000

6½ x 9 x 6 inches
(16.5 x 22.9 x 15.2 cm)
Wheel-thrown and altered
white stoneware; reduction
fired, cone 10; temmoku
and ash glazes
PHOTO BY MONICA RIPLEY

Diane Rosenmiller

Untitled, 2003

9 x 7 x 5 inches (22.9 x 17.8 x 12.7 cm)
Wheel-thrown and altered porcelain;
soda fired, cone 10

PHOTO BY NICHOLAS SEIDNER

Sheila Morissette

Wood-Fired Jug with Ash Drip, 2004

10 x 9½ x 5½ inches (25.4 x 24.1 x 14 cm)
Wheel-thrown and assembled stoneware; wood
fired, cone 10; exterior dipped in clay slip
PHOTO BY ALEXANDER DUFF

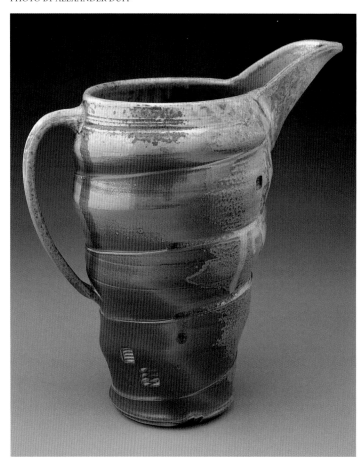

I am fortunate to live on the rugged West Coast, surrounded by the ocean and mountains, abundant with arbutus trees and large rock outcroppings. Wood firing captures the essence of my inspiration. The colors and textures of rugged rock are directly reflected on the pots after they emerge from the kiln. —SM

Kathy Phelps

Untitled, 2002

9 x 5½ x 3½ inches (22.9 x 14 x 8.9 cm)
Hand-built and textured earthenware;
electric fired, cone 6; stained with engobe
PHOTO BY WALKER MONTGOMERY

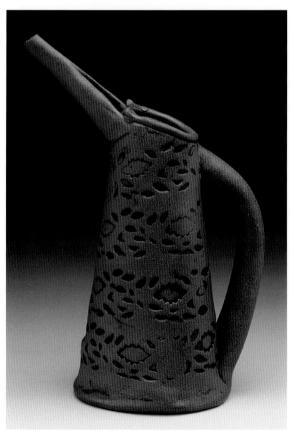

Conner Burns

Pitcher, 2005

9 x 12 x 7 inches (22.9 x 30.5 x 17.8 cm)
Wheel-thrown, altered, and slab-built white
stoneware; single fired in reduction, cone 10
PHOTO BY B.A. DEE

Kathryn Finnerty

Pitcher with Birds, 2004

10 x 7 inches (25.4 x 17.8 cm)
Hand- and slab-built terra cotta; electric
fired, cone 04; white slip, polychrome glazes,
raised-line decoration, sprigging, sgrafitto
PHOTO BY TOM ROHR

Elaine Pinkernell

Watering Can, 2003

9 x 11 x 3 inches (22.9 x 27.9 x 7.6 cm)
Slab-built stoneware; gas fired, cone 10;
soft-clay construction
PHOTO BY GEORGE POST

Ryan Forrey

Squared Pitcher, 2005

9 x 6 x 5 inches (22.9 x 15.2 x 12.7 cm)
Wheel-thrown porcelain; reduction fired,
cone 10; wood ash glazes
PHOTO BY ARTIST

Scott D. Cornish

Leaf Pitcher, 2004

8½ x 6 x 4½ inches (21.6 x 15.2 x 11.4 cm)
Wheel-thrown and altered porcelain; soda fired,
cone 11; ash glaze with wax resist
PHOTO BY ARTIST

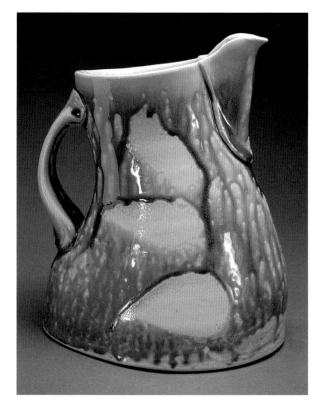

Debra E. Sloan

Dog Pitcher, 2005

20 x 7 x 7 inches (50.8 x 17.8 x 17.8 cm)
Slab-built red clay; electric fired, cone 01;
terra sigillata and colemanite wash

PHOTO BY TERRY YIP

Jennifer Everett

Pitcher, 2001

8 x 10½ x 6 inches (20.3 x 26.7 x 15.2 cm)
Wheel-thrown and assembled stoneware;
reduction fired, cone 10; stamped
decoration; glazes with wax resist
PHOTO BY ARTIST

Fred Johnston

Beaked Pitcher, 2000

10 x 6 x 3½ inches
(25.4 x 15.2 x 8.9 cm)
Wheel-thrown, altered, and
hand-built stoneware; wood
fired with salt and soda, cone
12; crackle slip, amber celadon
PHOTO BY ARTIST

Ron Boling

Pitcher, 2004

11 x 9 inches (27.9 x 22.9 cm)
Wheel-thrown; propane fired, cone 07;
raku fired in shredded-paper reduction
PHOTO BY DEAN JONES

Charlie Tefft

Untitled, 2002

10 x 5½ x 5 inches (24.5 x 14 x 12.7 cm)
Wheel-thrown and altered white stoneware;
gas fired, cone 10; multiple ash glazes

Pat Blackwelder

Untitled, 2005

8¾ x 6 inches (22.2 x 15.2 cm)
Wheel-thrown stoneware; reduction fired, cone 10
PHOTO BY SCOTT LYKENS

David W. Scott

Untitled, 2005

9 x 9 x 7 inches (22.9 x 22.9 x 17.8 cm)
Wheel-thrown porcelain; reduction fired,
cone 10; sprayed matte glazes
PHOTO BY ARTIST

Blair Clemo

Pitcher with Pink Roses, 2005

5 x 7 x 4 inches (12.7 x 17.8 x 10.2 cm)
Wheel-thrown porcelain; oxidation fired,
cone 7; stamped underglaze, decals
PHOTO BY CHRIS AUTIO

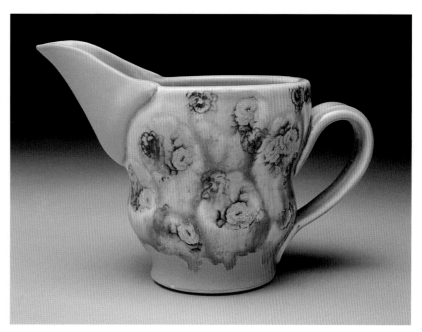

Carol B. Eder

Untitled, 2005

4 x 5 x 3 inches (10.2 x 12.7 x 7.6 cm)
Wheel-thrown and hand-built porcelain;
electric fired in oxidation, cone 9
PHOTO BY TONY DECK

Anne Fallis Elliott

| *Low Pitcher*, 2000

5 x 9 x 3½ inches (12.7 x 22.9 x 8.9 cm)
Wheel-thrown, altered, and assembled white
stoneware; electric fired, cone 7; ash glaze
PHOTO BY KEVIN NOBLE

There's a subtle sophistication in Anne Fallis Elliott's pitcher. The thin slab
construction seems direct and immediate, with many subtle qualities evident,
and her black glaze contributes to the spare and understated form. —*TG*

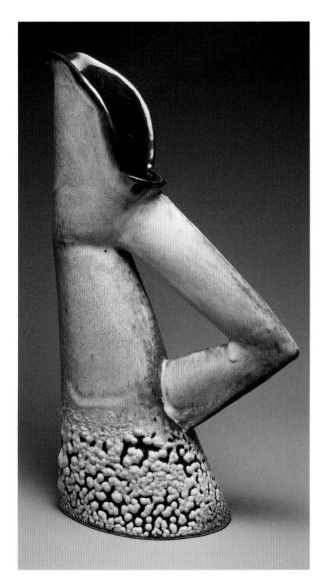

Bacia Edelman

Tall Pitcher, 2003

17 x 14 x 6 inches (43.2 x 35.6 x 15.2 cm)
Slab-constructed stoneware; electric fired,
cone 6; vitreous engobe under semi-matte
and lichen glaze, gloss interior
PHOTO BY ARTIST

Vijay V. Paniker

Black Pitcher, 2005

9½ x 8½ x 8½ inches (24.1 x 21.6 x 21.6 cm)
Wheel-thrown stoneware; gas fired, cone 10
PHOTO BY ANDREA M. ALLEN

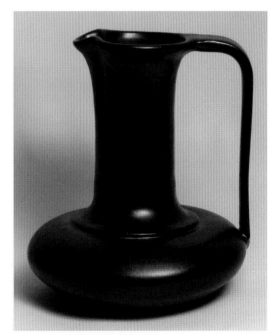

Jan Stackhouse

Untitled, 2002

8 x 5½ x 2½ inches (20.3 x 14 x 6.4 cm)
Hand-built and stamped earthenware;
electric fired, cone 02; underglazes;
clear overglaze, cone 05

PHOTO BY ELIZABETH ELLINGSON
COURTESY OF HANSON-HOWARD GALLERY,
ASHLAND, OREGON

Emily Dyer

Polka Dot Pitcher, 2005

8 x 6½ x 6 inches (20.3 x 16.5 x 15.2 cm)
Wheel-thrown Laguna clay; reduction
fired, cone 10; layered glazes with
wax resist design
PHOTO BY PETRONELLA J. YTSMA

Repeating marks make patterns on the surface of a pot. Emily Dyer uses a simple wax relief circle motif to great effect, while Jan Stackhouse incorporates a central panel with repeating spirals in the background of this active motif. *—TG*

Jill J. Burns

Beverage Pitcher, 2005

12 x 7 x 6 inches (30.5 x 17.8 x 15.2 cm)
Wheel-thrown and assembled; soda
fired, cone 10
PHOTO BY ARTIST

Nathan Falter

Untitled, 2005

10 x 7 x 5 inches (25.4 x 17.8 x 12.7 cm)
Wheel-thrown and altered
stoneware; electric fired, cone 6;
terra sigillata, oxides
PHOTO BY ARTIST

Todd Holmberg

Pitcher, 2005

7 x 5 x 4 inches (17.8 x 12.7 x 10.2 cm)
Wheel-thrown and altered stoneware;
reduction fired, cone 10
PHOTO BY PETER LEE

Brad Schwieger

Soda-Fired Pitcher, 2004

18 x 7 x 7 inches (45.7 x 17.8 x 17.8 cm)
Wheel-thrown stoneware; soda fired,
cone 10; flashing slip
PHOTO BY ARTIST

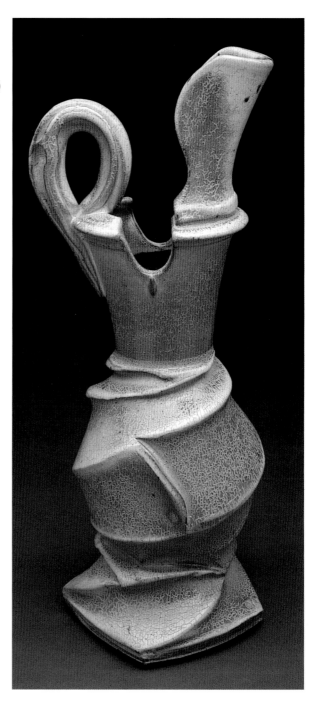

Mike Meyer

Leaf Pitcher, 2004

10 x 8 x 2½ inches
(25.4 x 20.3 x 6.4 cm)
Slab-built stoneware; bisque fired,
cone 08; red iron stain, cone 7
PHOTO BY DAVID EGAN

Mike Meyer has
made the difficult
look easy in his
marriage of handle
with spout, form
with surface. He
has taken a simple
leaf impression
technique and
worked it into a
complex but
pleasing pattern.

—TG

Mark Branstine

What's It To Ya?, 2005

13 x 9 x 5 inches (33 x 22.9 x 12.7 cm)
Slab-built porcelain; gas fired in reduction,
cone 10; celadon glaze with red underglaze
and overspray; white liner glaze
PHOTO BY ARTIST

Many potters seek to
discover or create ways of
working and developing
forms that are unique to
their individual sensibility.
With Mark Branstine's
approach, the transparent
green glaze is a quiet
setting for the particulars
of his complex
construction. —*TG*

Steven Zoldak

Pitcher, 2003

7 x 7 x 5 inches (17.8 x 17.8 x 12.7 cm)
Wheel-thrown and carved stoneware;
gas fired in reduction, cone 10
PHOTO BY CHARLEY FREIBERG

Tracy Shell

Pitcher, 2005

10½ x 6½ x 5 inches (26.7 x 16.5 x 12.7 cm)
Wheel-thrown porcelain; electric fired, cone 6
PHOTO BY ARTIST

Laurel MacDuffie

Small Pitcher and Tray, 2003

Pitcher: 4½ x 4 x 3 inches (11.4 x 10.2 x 7.6 cm);
Tray: 3¾ inches in diameter (9.5 cm)
Wheel-thrown stoneware; cone 10; salt
and ash glaze
PHOTO BY ARTIST

Carole Ann Fer

Pitcher, 2004

6 x 4½ x 2½ inches (15.2 x 11.4 x 6.4)
Wheel-thrown and altered porcelain;
oxidation fired, cone 6; satin matte
glaze, copper wash
PHOTO BY ELLEN WIESKE

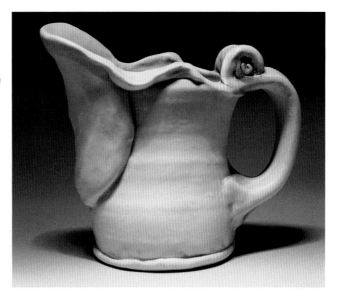

Marsha Karagheusian

Petite Pour, 2005

7½ x 8 x 3½ inches (19 x 20.3 x 8.9 cm)
Hand-built and textured earthenware;
electric fired, cone 06; multiple stains;
pit fired in straw and sawdust
PHOTO BY MEL MITTERMILLER

Lisa Buck

Amber Pitcher, 2004

9½ x 6 x 6 inches (24.1 x 15.2 x 15.2 cm)
Wheel-thrown earthenware; electric
fired, cone 04
PHOTO BY STEVE SCHNEIDER

Linda Arbuckle

| *Pitcher: Summer With Bleeding Hearts,* 2003

7½ x 5 x 6 inches (19 x 12.7 x 15.2 cm)
Wheel-thrown and altered terra cotta;
electric fired, cone 03; majolica glaze
PHOTO BY ARTIST

Gloria Singer

| Untitled, 2004

5¼ x 6 x 3¾ inches (13.3 x 15.2 x 9.5 cm)
Wheel-thrown and altered stoneware clay;
electric fired, cone 6½
PHOTO BY ARTIST

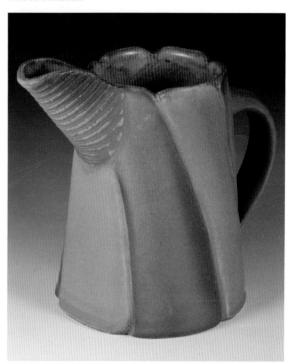

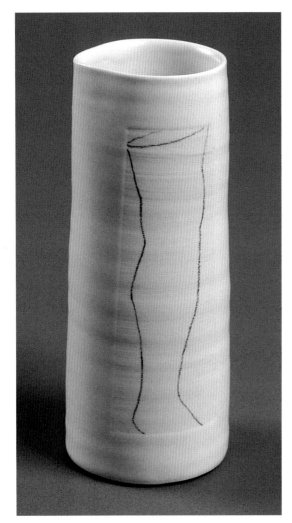

Lois Harbaugh

Hollow Leg, 2005

7¼ x 3 x 3 inches (18.4 x 7.6 x 7.6 cm)
Wheel-thrown porcelain; gas fired,
cone 10; glaze pencil drawing,
electric fired, cone 05
PHOTO BY RICHARD NICHOL

In this minimalist pitcher, the soft columnar shape
of the vessel is similar to the organic asymmetry
of a turned leg. The phrase "hollow leg" connotes
infinite retaining capacity, whereas "pitcher"
brings to mind pouring or emptying. —*LH*

Amy Higgason

Untitled, 2004

9½ x 6⅜ x 4¾ inches (24.1 x 16.2 x 12.1 cm)
Wheel-thrown white stoneware with additions; electric
fired, cone 6; carved, impressed, sprig decoration
PHOTO BY GUY NICOL

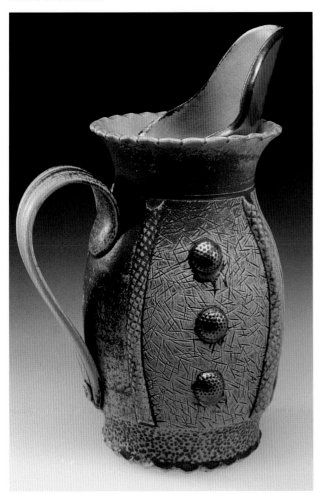

Rachel Bleil

Ribbed Pitcher, 2005

9 x 8 x 5 inches (22.9 x 20.3 x 12.7 cm)
Hand-built white earthenware; electric
fired, cone 04; terra sigillata, stains, glazes
PHOTO BY ARTIST

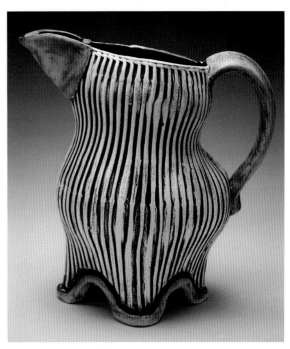

Shannon Nelson

Syrup Pitcher, 2000

5¼ x 5 x 3½ inches (13.3 x 12.7 x 8.9 cm)
Thrown, altered, and hand-built porcelain;
electric fired in oxidation, cone 6
PHOTO BY JOHN KNAUB

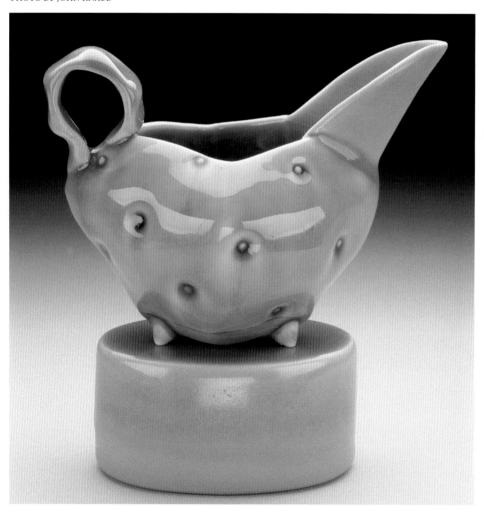

Every pitcher has its own poise or stance, be it regal and upright or dynamic and gestural. Shannon Nelson's *Syrup Pitcher* achieves much of its personality through the sum of its parts, including its apricot-colored perch. —*TG*

Kimberly Rorick

Flower Swirl Pitcher, 2001

7 x 8 x 3½ inches (17.8 x 20.3 x 8.9 cm)
Wheel-thrown and altered porcelain;
electric fired, cone 6; hand-painted
slips and underglaze
PHOTO BY JOHN ESCOSA

Claudia Zeber-Martell
Michael Zeber-Martell

| Untitled, 2004

8 x 11 x 6 inches (20.3 x 27.9 x 15.2 cm)
Wheel-thrown and altered white earthenware;
electric fired, cone 06; airbrushed and brush-
textured Mason stains, gloss glaze finish
PHOTO BY JIM MARTIN

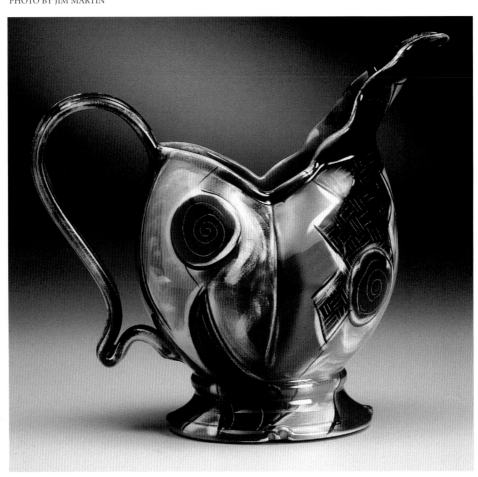

Anne Bernard-Pattis

Forest Fairies, 2004

8 x 6 inches (20.3 x 15.2 cm)
Wheel-thrown porcelain; gas fired,
cone 10; celadon glaze
PHOTOS BY WILLIAM BIDERBOST

Steven Zoldak

Creamer, 2004

4 x 4 x 3 inches (10.2 x 10.2 x 7.6 cm)
Wheel-thrown and altered stoneware; gas
fired in reduction, cone 10; slip decoration
PHOTO BY CHARLEY FREIBERG

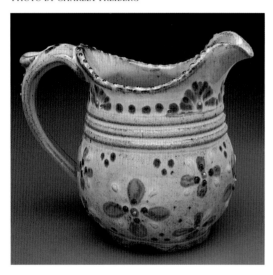

Theresa Puffer

Cornflower Blue, 2005

7½ x 8 x 5½ inches (19 x 20.3 x 14 cm)
Wheel-thrown earthenware; electric fired,
cone 04; low-fire underglaze and glaze
PHOTO BY PETER LEE

Barry W. Gregg

Grandma's Pattern, 2003

15 x 9 x 5 inches (38.1 x 22.9 x 12.7 cm)
Slab and coil-built stoneware; salt fired,
cone 6; slips and glazes

PHOTO BY WALKER MONTGOMERY

Stephanie Osser

My Flutist, 2003

5¾ x 5 x 4 inches (14.6 x 12.7 x 10.2 cm)
Modeled clay figure on thrown pitcher;
four-part mold; slip cast and bisque fired,
cone 04; underglazes, clear glaze, cone 06
PHOTO BY DAVID CARAS

The tradition of figurative ceramics is as ancient as civilization itself. Stephanie Osser's pitcher contributes to this legacy with its seated individual poised to play as well as to pour. —*TG*

Tanya R. Mercado Lang

Ready, Set, Pounce!, 2005

4½ x 7¾ x 3 inches (11.4 x 19.7 x 7.6 cm)
Wheel-thrown and hand-built red clay;
electric fired, cone 6

PHOTO BY RICHARD NICKEL AND ARTIST

Karen Copensky

Cape Buffalo Ewer, 2004

5½ x 10 x 4 inches (14 x 25.4 x 10.2 cm)
Hand-built and pinched stoneware;
wood fired in anagama kiln, cone 12;
natural ash glaze

PHOTO BY CRAIG PHILLIPS

Pia Sillem

North-West, 2003

13 x 7½ x 5¼ inches (33 x 19.1 x 13.3 cm)
Wheel-thrown and altered stoneware; wood
fired in anagama kiln, cone 13
PHOTO BY ALEXANDER DUFF

Nancy Button

Tree Pitcher, 2004

11 x 5 x 7 inches (27.9 x 12.7 x 17.8 cm)
Bark-textured, slab-built stoneware;
wood fired, cone 10

Do-Hee Sung

Green Bamboo Pitcher, 2004

9 x 8 x 4 inches (22.9 x 20.3 x 10.2 cm)
Wheel-thrown and altered stoneware;
reduction fired, cone 10; wax resist

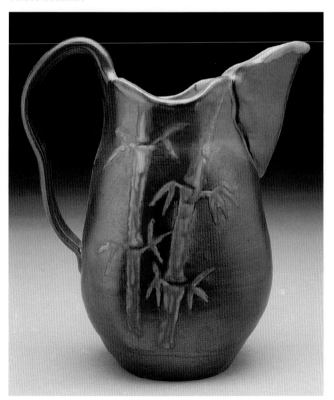

500 PITCHERS

Anne Goldberg

Altered Pitcher, 2003

6 x 6 x 4 inches (15.2 x 15.2 x 10.2 cm)
Wheel-thrown and altered porcelain; reduction
fired, cone 10; shino glaze
PHOTO BY ARTIST

Michael Kline

Pitcher, 2004

10 x 10 x 8 inches (25.4 x 25.4 x 20.3 cm)
Wheel-thrown and darted stoneware; wood
fired with salt, cone 10; wax resist, black slip
PHOTO BY WALKER MONTGOMERY

Carole Ann Fer

Pass the Gravy Please, 2004

8 x 6 x 3 inches (20.3 x 15.2 x 7.6 cm) overall
Wheel-thrown and altered porcelain;
oxidation fired, cone 6; satin matte glaze,
copper wash, sgraffito
PHOTO BY ELLEN WIESKE

Christy Wetzig

Striped Rocking Pitcher, 2005

7 x 9 x 4 inches (17.8 x 22.9 x 10.2 cm)
White stoneware; cone 10; wax resist,
soda and ash glaze
PHOTO BY PETER LEE

Lynn Fisher

Burdock Pitcher, 2003

7 x 6 x 5 inches (17.8 x 15.2 x 12.7 cm)
Hand-built stoneware; electric fired,
cone 9; impressed and joined leaf slabs
PHOTO BY STEVE KOSTYSHYN

Charity Davis-Woodard

Long-Beaked Pitcher with Bead, 2003

14 x 8 x 5½ inches (35.6 x 20.3 x 14 cm)
Wheel-thrown porcelain with slab spout; wood
fired in Bourry box kiln, cone 10; porcelain
bead, Nichrome wire
PHOTO BY TONY DECK

Nathan Carris Carnes

Untitled, 2004

13 x 9 x 9 inches (33 x 22.9 x 22.9 cm)
Wheel-thrown stoneware; wood fired, cone 12
PHOTO BY ARTIST

Bradley Keys

Untitled, 2005

8½ x 5½ x 7 inches (22 x 14 x 18 cm)
Wheel-thrown and altered red stoneware;
electric fired, cone 6; multiple sprayed glazes
PHOTO BY ARTIST

Adama Sow

Shino Pitcher, 2005

10½ x 6 inches (26.7 x 15.2 cm)
Wheel-thrown stoneware; gas fired,
cone 10; shino glaze
PHOTO BY PETER LEE

Shawn Ireland

Pitcher, 2004

Height: 10 inches (25.4 cm)
Stoneware; wood fired,
cone 9 to 10; ash glaze
PHOTO BY WALKER MONTGOMERY

Shawn Ireland has clearly designed this stately pitcher with usefulness in mind. The belly's capacity is inviting but not showy, the handle well integrated into the form, and the lip sturdy and ready to pour. —*TG*

Andy Porter

Walking Jug, 2004

8¾ x 5¾ x 7 inches (22.2 x 14.6 x 17.8 cm)
Wheel-thrown porcelain, modeled feet, pulled
and split handle; gas fired, cone 10
PHOTO BY GENNA GRUSHOVENKO

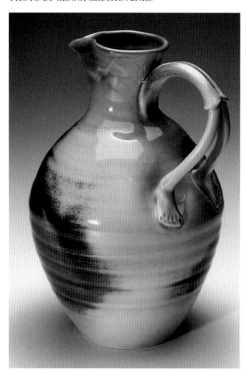

Loren Lukens

Pitcher, 2002

11 x 9 x 5 inches (27.9 x 22.9 x 12.7 cm)
Slip-cast and hand-built porcelain; reduction
fired, cone 10; multiple sprayed glazes
PHOTO BY ARTIST

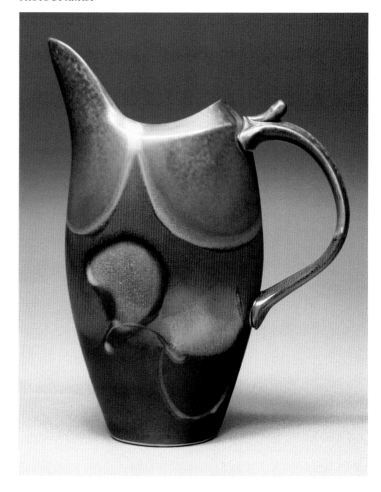

Laura O'Donnell

Fish Motif Pitcher, 2005

9 x 6½ x 5 inches (22.9 x 16.5 x 12.7 cm)
Wheel-thrown stoneware; gas fired in
reduction, cone 10; matte glaze, black
slip decoration
PHOTO BY CHRIS BERTI

When making vessels,
I think about them first in
terms of decoration and
then produce a form that
complements it. The form
of this pitcher echoes
the shape of the fish
on its surface. —*LO*

Rachel Berg

Untitled, 2003

10 x 5 x 5½ inches (25.4 x 12.7 x 14 cm)
Wheel-thrown and hand-built stoneware;
reduction fired, cone 10; impressed designs
PHOTO BY ARTIST

Lowell T. Hoisington II

Sunset Pitcher, 2000

8¾ x 5 x 6 inches (22.2 x 12.7 x 15.2 cm)
Wheel-thrown stoneware; wood fired
with light salt, cone 10; flashing slip,
stain, celadon glaze
PHOTO BY ARTIST

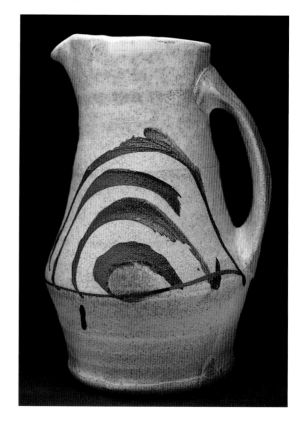

Marion Schlauch

Lizard Pitcher, 2000

15 inches (38.1 cm)
Wheel-thrown white stoneware;
wood fired in anagama kiln, cone 12;
shino glaze
PHOTO BY ROBERT BATEY

Adama Sow

Bogoland, 2005

10½ x 6½ inches (26.7 x 16.5 cm)
Wheel-thrown stoneware; electric fired,
cone 6; glaze
PHOTO BY PETER LEE

My art is influenced by the traditional potters of Senegal and by my experiences in Europe and America. I try to combine African techniques with those from the United States or Europe. —AS

Valerie Metcalfe

> *Midnight Blue Pitcher*, 2001

10 x 5 inches (25.4 x 12.7 cm)
Wheel-thrown and carved porcelain; gas fired in
reduction, cone 11; wax resist design
PHOTO BY BRUCE SPIELMAN

Michéle C. Drivon

> *Purple Pitcher*, 2003

9½ x 6½ x 3¼ inches (24.1 x 16.5 x 8.3 cm)
Wheel-thrown porcelain; electric fired, cone 6
PHOTO BY ROBERT GIBSON

Linda McFarling

Untitled, 2004

6 x 7 x 6 inches (15.2 x 17.8 x 15.2 cm)
Wheel-thrown stoneware; soda fired, cone 10
PHOTO BY TOM MILLS

Debra P. Holiber

Untitled, 2004

11 x 7 x 5 inches (27.9 x 17.8 x 12.7 cm)
Wheel-thrown, altered, and assembled
porcelain; reduction fired, cone 10
PHOTOS BY LOREN MARON

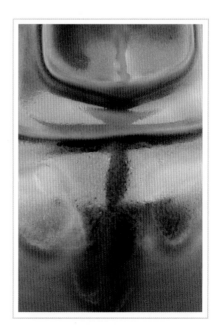

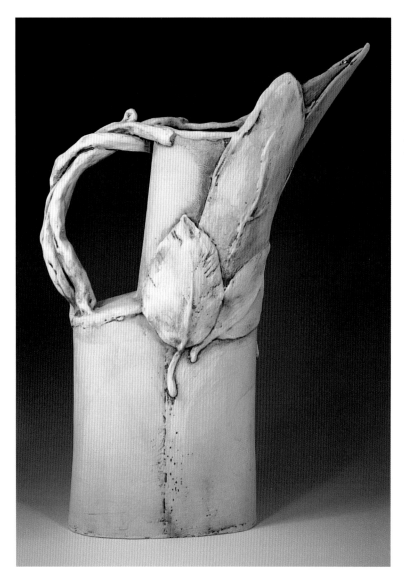

Leaf Pitcher #5, 2005

15 x 11 x 3 inches (38.1 x 27.9 x 7.6 cm)
Hand-built, low-fire clay; multiple firings,
cones 06 to 04; layered engobes, oxide, and
glaze washes
PHOTOS BY ARTIST

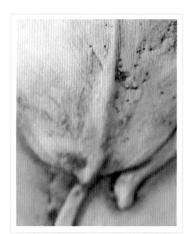

The objects encountered in daily activities directly influenced this piece.
I've always been inspired by the beauty and endless variety of natural
forms. The geometric simplicity in the body of this pitcher provides a stark
and understated background for more complex and textured attachments
in the shapes of tree branches or other forms of vegetation. —*UM*

Maemi Kathleen Matsushita

| *Blooming Irises*, 2001

9 x 6½ x 5½ inches (22.9 x 16.5 x 14 cm)
Wheel-thrown and incised porcelain; electric
fired, cone 6; underglazes, clear glaze

PHOTO BY DALE RODDICK

Warren Moyer

| *Pitcher*, 2005

12 x 8 x 4 inches (30.5 x 20.3 x 10.2 cm)
Slab-built stoneware; reduction fired,
cone 10; glaze, sgrafitto

PHOTO BY SCOTT LYKENS

Made in Detroit, 2003

12 x 3¼ x 8 inches (30.5 x 8.3 x 20.3 cm)
Slab-built stoneware; electric fired, cone 6
PHOTO BY ARTIST

Bacia Edelman

White Ewer, 2004

5 x 5½ x 3 inches (12.7 x 14 x 7.6 cm)
Wheel-thrown, hand-built, cut, and
assembled porcelain; wood fired, cone
11; matte glaze
PHOTO BY ARTIST

Sandra Shaughnessy

Beak Pitcher, 2005

7½ x 12½ x 4 inches
(19 x 31.8 x 10.2 cm)
Wheel-thrown and altered white
stoneware; soda fired, cone 10;
flashing slips, glaze, underglaze
PHOTO BY PETRONELLA YTSMA

Frank James Fisher

Newspaper Pitcher, 2005

11½ x 4 x 4 inches (29.2 x 10.2 x 10.2 cm)
Slab-built porcelain; raku fired; metal and
cardboard handle attached with hemp cord
PHOTO BY ARTIST

Kathy Phelps

Untitled, 2005

8 x 6 x 3 inches (20.3 x 15.2 x 7.6 cm)
Wheel-thrown and altered white
stoneware; cone 6; slip and underglaze
decoration; salt glaze
PHOTOS BY DREW STAUSS

Kathy Lorenz

Pitcher, 2002

9 x 9 x 7 inches (22.9 x 22.9 x 17.8 cm)
Wheel-thrown and altered porcelain;
soda fired, cone 10
PHOTO BY ARTIST

Emily Murphy

Midwestern Creamer, 2003

5½ x 5 x 2½ inches (14 x 12.7 x 6.4 cm)
Wheel-thrown and altered stoneware;
reduction fired with soda, cone 10; dipped
in flashing slip, brushwork
PHOTO BY GUY NICOL

Do-Hee Sung

Orchid Pitcher, 2005

7 x 5 x 3 inches (17.8 x 12.7 x 7.6 cm)
Wheel-thrown and altered porcelain;
electric fired, cone 6; drawing, stencil
motifs; gold luster, cone 018
PHOTO BY ARTIST

Marian Baker

Pitcher with Stripes, 2004

8 x 6 x 4 inches (20.3 x 15.2 x 10.2 cm)
Wheel-thrown and altered porcelain;
electric fired, cone 6

PHOTOS BY ARTIST

Joe Bova
Kristen Kieffer

❙ *Pitcher*, 2001

9¼ x 8 x 4½ inches
(23.5 x 20.3 x 11.4 cm)
Wheel-thrown and altered white
stoneware; soda fired, cone 10;
stamped and slip-trailed (Kieffer),
hand-built additions (Bova)
PHOTOS BY ARTISTS

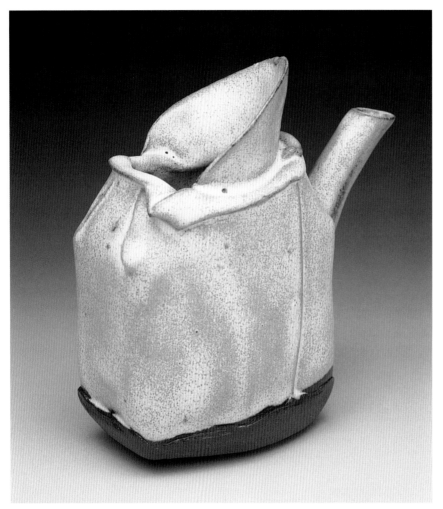

Shouyu Pitcher, 2001

4½ x 3 x 2 inches (11.4 x 7.6 x 5 cm)
Slab- and coil-built stoneware;
electric fired, cone 6
PHOTO BY LUIS GARCIA

There's a modesty of scale and technique in Heather O'Brien's
ewer that is quite endearing. She has left in view evidence of the
slab construction process, choosing to reveal her method and
make it part of the personality of the finished pot. —*TG*

Jordan Taylor

Untitled, 2004

14 x 7 x 6 inches (35.6 x 17.8 x 15.2 cm)
Wheel-thrown stoneware; wood fired, cone 10
PHOTO BY LESLI VANZANDENBERGEN

Von Venhuizen

Funnel Included, 2005

12 x 12 x 10 inches (30.5 x 30.5 x 25.4 cm)
Slip-cast porcelain; reduction fired, cone 1;
colored slips with oxide wash
PHOTOS BY ARTIST

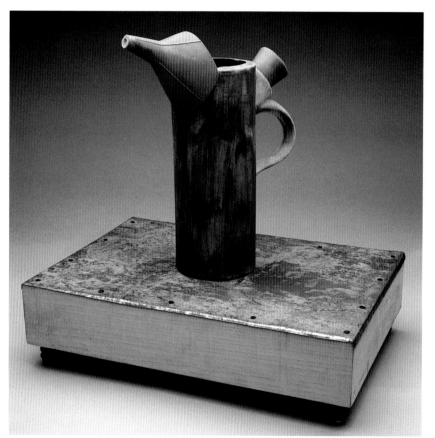

Caroline Holder

A Woman's Hair Is Her Crowning Glory, 2005

15 x 8 x 5 inches (38.1 x 20.3 x 12.7 cm)
Hand-built porcelain; electric fired, cone 6; sgrafitto
PHOTOS BY D. JAMES DEE

Many of my narrative pieces center on themes of home and belonging, or contain commentary on growing up in Barbados. This piece contains a comment on the insane practice of straightening hair with a hot metal comb. —*CH*

Bonnie Belt

Branch Pitcher, 2004

12 x 10 x 6 inches (30.5 x 25.4 x 15.2 cm)
Wheel-thrown and hand-sculpted white
stoneware; propane fired, cone 3;
airbrushed underglaze, smoke-fired finish
PHOTO BY HAP SAKWA

David Irish

Untitled, 2005

20 x 8 x 8 inches (50.8 x 20.3 x 20.3 cm)
Wheel-thrown stoneware; reduction
fired, cone 10

PHOTOS BY PROFESSOR MARVIN BJURLIN

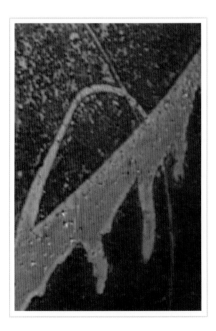

Jon Arsenault

Pitcher Pair, 2000

9 x 6 inches each (22.9 x 15.2 cm)
Stoneware; salt fired, cone 10;
colored slips and glazes
PHOTO BY ARTIST

Jenny Lou Sherburne

Etruscan Pitcher, 1996

18 x 14 x 14 inches (45.7 x 35.6 x 35.6 cm)
Coil-built stoneware; electric fired, cones
04 and 06; additions, engobes, glazes
PHOTO BY STEVE MELTZER

There is a tradition in ceramics of what could be called "palace ware"—ornate, exotic vessels that were meant to appoint and exalt the wealthy prestige of the monarchy. Jenny Lou Sherburne's floral exotica are reminiscent of those types of exuberant, celebratory pitchers. —*TG*

David Pier

Pitcher, Style # 3, 2003

9 x 8 x 10 inches (22.9 x 20.3 x 25.4 cm)
Slip-cast porcelain; reduction fired, cone 10
PHOTO BY ARTIST

Kazu Oba

Sake Pitcher, 2004

Pitcher: 3 x 6 x 5 inches (7.6 x 15.2 x 12.7 cm)
Wheel-thrown stoneware; electric fired, cone 6
PHOTOS BY ARTIST

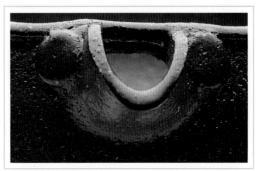

Chris Gray

| Untitled, 2005

10 x 7 x 9½ inches (25.4 x 17.8 x 24.1 cm)
Wheel-thrown porcelain; electric fired,
cone 10; wax resist
PHOTO BY ARTIST

Chris Gray unifies
form and surface
with a careful
wax resist pattern
between two
rich glazes. —TG

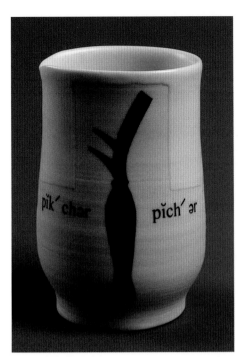

Lois Harbaugh

| *The Enunciation*, 2005

4½ x 3 x 2½ inches (11.4 x 7.6 x 6.4 cm)
Wheel-thrown porcelain; gas fired, cone 10;
underglaze imagery, electric fired, cone 05
PHOTO BY RICHARD NICHOL

I derive a lot of pleasure from word play, so I made a piece about
the phonetic distinction between the words "pitcher" and "picture."
The silhouetted image is one of my double-spouted pitchers. —*LH*

Do-Hee Sung

| *Buncheong Creamer*, 2005

3 x 6 x 3 inches (7.6 x 15.2 x 7.6 cm)
Wheel-thrown and altered porcelain;
electric fired, cone 6; sgrafitto,
Buncheong-style slip, carving;
mother-of-pearl, cone 019
PHOTO BY ARTIST

Jeff Brown

Carafe, 2003

11 x 8 x 8 inches (27.9 x 20.3 x 20.3 cm)
Thrown and textured stoneware; wood
fired, cone 10; shino glaze
PHOTO BY ARTIST

I am drawn to the natural earth
qualities of clay: the smell, the look,
the feel of its granular surface as
it's stretched by the pressure of my
fingertips. My fascination with
texture and the pliable nature of
clay leads me to examine, not just
the outside, the skin, but within the
clay, below the surface. I challenge
myself by finding new ways to
better express and use these
elements in my work. I find the
historical uses of clay, wood, metal,
and stone valuable resources, but
nothing speaks to me more clearly
than clay itself and how it responds
to manipulation. —JB

Lucia Ramenzoni

| Untitled, 1995

9½ x 7⅞ inches (24 x 20 cm)
Wheel-thrown stoneware; gas fired, cone 10
PHOTO BY LU CRISTOVAM

Forrest Lesch-Middelton

| *Soda-Fired Pitcher,* 2004

10 x 7 inches (25.4 x 17.8 cm)
Stoneware; soda fired, cone 10
PHOTO BY ARTIST

Mark Strom

Pitcher with a Jaunty Tilt, 2005

5¼ x 8½ x 4¼ inches (13.3 x 21.6 x 10.8 cm)
Wheel-thrown and slab-built porcelain; reduction
fired, cone 10; layered stains and glazes
PHOTO BY RICHARD NICOL

Nicole Copel

| Untitled, 2004

6½ x 5 x 4 inches (16.5 x 12.7 x 10.2 cm)
Wheel-thrown porcelain; electric fired, cone 6;
variation on Lana Wilson's Aqua Bronze glaze
PHOTO BY ARTIST

Rachel Berg

| Untitled, 2004

5½ x 4½ x 3 inches (14 x 11.4 x 7.6 cm)
Wheel-thrown and hand-built stoneware; soda fired,
cone 10; impressed designs
PHOTO BY ARTIST

Charity Davis-Woodard

Pitcher with Rope Texture, 2004

8 x 7 x 6 inches (20.3 x 17.8 x 15.2 cm)
Wheel-thrown porcelain; wood fired in Bourry box kiln, cone 10
PHOTO BY TONY DECK

Shino Water Jug, 2005

7½ x 8½ x 4½ inches
(19 x 21.6 x 11.4 cm)
Wheel-thrown and altered
stoneware; gas fired in
reduction, cone 10
PHOTOS BY ARTIST

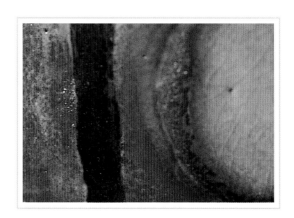

David Pier

Creamer, 1996

4½ x 3 x 4¼ inches (11.4 x 7.6 x 10.8 cm)
Hand-built stoneware; reduction fired, cone 10
PHOTO BY ARTIST

Brian Kovachik

Untitled, 2005

8 x 5½ x 4½ inches (20.3 x 14 x 11.4 cm)
Wheel-thrown white stoneware;
wood fired, cone 13
PHOTO BY ARTIST

Clarice Ann Dorst

Raku Pitcher, 2003

12½ x 9½ x 4 inches (31.8 x 24.1 x 10.2 cm)
Wheel-thrown and assembled stoneware; gas
fired in raku kiln; Crusty Dusty glaze
PHOTO BY ARTIST

Penny Sharp Sky

| Untitled, 2004

10 x 9 x 8 inches (25.4 x 22.9 x 20.3 cm)
Slab-built stoneware; gas fired in
reduction, cone 11
PHOTO BY ARTIST

Charlie Blosser

| Untitled, 2003

16½ x 5½ inches (41.9 x 14 cm)
Wheel-thrown stoneware; electric
fired, cone 6
PHOTO BY ANNE MCCARTHY

Martha H. Grover

Two Pitchers, 2004

10 x 12 x 3 inches each
(25.4 x 30.5 x 7.6 cm)
Wheel-thrown and altered porcelain; soda
fired, cone 10
PHOTO BY ARTIST

Connie Christensen

Untitled, 2005

4½ x 4 x 3 inches (11.4 x 10.2 x 7.6 cm)
Wheel-thrown and altered porcelain;
reduction fired, cone 10; Malcolm's
Shino glaze
PHOTO BY KAZU OBA

Elise Hauenstein

Pitcher, 2003

7¼ x 7¼ x 4 inches (18.4 x 18.4 x 10.2 cm)
Wheel-thrown and altered white stoneware;
reduction fired, cone 10; sprayed glaze
PHOTO BY MONICA RIPLEY

Tim Ludwig

Pitcher with Agen Tulip, 2004

25 x 16 x 14 inches (63.5 x 40.6 x 35.6 cm)
Wheel-thrown earthenware; electric fired,
cone 05; Mason stains and slips
PHOTO BY RANDY SMITH

Adrienne Dellinger

Lidded Pitcher, 2004

9 x 5½ x 3½ inches (22.9 x 14 x 8.9 cm)
Wheel-thrown stoneware; electric fired, cone 6
PHOTO BY JIM KAMMER

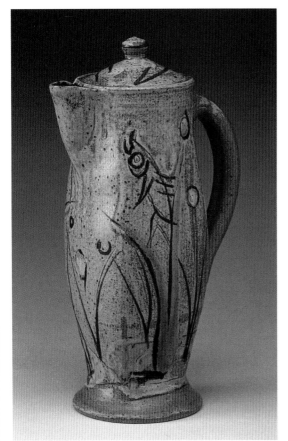

Posey Bacopoulos

Gravy Pitcher, 2005

5 x 9 x 4 inches (12.7 x 22.9 x 10.2 cm)
Thrown, altered, and assembled terra cotta; electric
fired, cone 04; majolica and terra sigillata
PHOTO BY KEVIN NOBLE

Posey Bacopoulos brings her interest and flair with brushwork to bear on a simple pattern with a hint of contrasting motif under the spout. Her mark making is fresh, and the underlying logic of the pattern secondary to the informal irregularities of her brushwork. —*TG*

Adrienne Dellinger

Sauceboat, 2004

4 x 6 x 4 inches (10.2 x 15.2 x 10.2 cm)
Wheel-thrown and altered stoneware;
electric fired, cone 6
PHOTO BY JIM KAMMER

Gertrude Graham Smith

Gravy Boat, 2003

4½ x 6 x ¼ inches (11.4 x 15.2 x 0.6 cm)
Wheel-thrown and altered porcelain;
single fired with soda, cone 10
PHOTO BY TOM MILLS

Eloise Hally

Lemonade Set, 2004

Set: 9 x 12 x 10 inches (22.9 x 30.5 x 25.4 cm)
Wheel-thrown stoneware pitcher and cups,
slab-built tray; gas fired in reduction, cone 10
PHOTO BY BART KASTEN

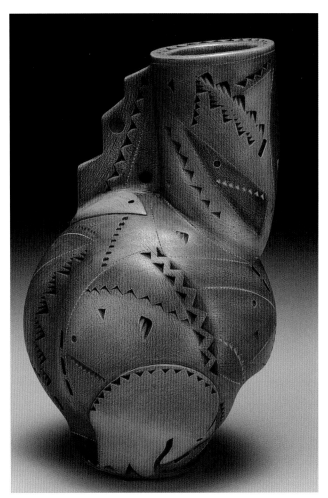

George Handy

Animals Come to Mind, 2004

8½ x 6 x 5 ½ inches (21.6 x 15.2 x 14 cm)
Wheel-thrown and altered porcelain;
oxidation fired, cone 6; celadon glaze,
low-fire stains, oxide pigment washes
PHOTO BY TIM BARNWELL

Lea Zoltowski

Bubble Pitcher, 2003

11 x 8 x 5 inches (27.9 x 20.3 x 12.7 cm)
Hand-built porcelain; wood fired, cone 10
PHOTO BY ARTIST

Rachel Berg

Untitled, 2003

11 x 6 x 5 inches (27.9 x 15.2 x 12.7 cm)
Wheel-thrown and hand-built stoneware;
reduction fired, cone 10; impressed design
PHOTO BY ARTIST

Cheyenne Chapman

Pitcher Set, 2004

7 x 5 x 4 inches each (17.8 x 12.7 x 10.2 cm)
Wheel-thrown and altered porcelain; fired in
oxidation with soda, cone 10
PHOTOS BY ARTIST

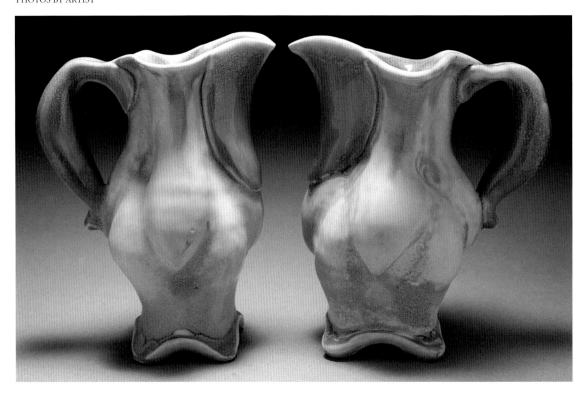

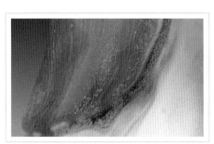

Dot Kolentsis

Untitled, 1997

7⅞ x 5⅛ x 4¾ inches (20 x 13 x 12 cm)
Wheel-thrown white earthenware; underglaze;
fired 2012°F (1100°C); clear gloss glaze
PHOTO BY JENNI CARTER

Susan Sheets

Rooster and Hen Pitcher, 2005

6 x 6⅛ x 4¼ inches (15.2 x 15.6 x 10.8 cm)
Wheel-thrown and altered white stoneware;
soda fired, cone 10; underglaze design on bisque
PHOTO BY PETRONELLA YTSMA

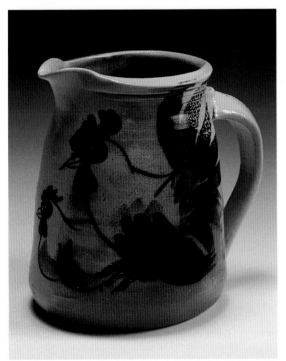

Christa Assad

Red Square Pitcher, 2004

9 x 7 x 5 inches (22.9 x 17.8 x 12.7 cm)
Wheel-thrown and hand-built stoneware;
electric fired, cone 6; masked and
wax-resist decoration
PHOTO BY WILFRED J. JONES

Kristin Schoonover

Striped Pitcher, 2005

11 x 9 x 8 inches (27.9 x 22.9 x 20.3 cm)
Wheel-thrown and altered white stoneware;
electric fired, cone 6
PHOTO BY ARTIST

Cat Jarosz

| *Large Pitcher,* 2002

13¼ x 5¼ x 6⅞ inches (33.7 x 13.3 x 17.5 cm)
Wheel-thrown, altered, and pulled stoneware;
gas fired in reduction, cones 10 to 12
PHOTO BY TIM BARNWELL

Adam Sterrett

Ash Glaze Pitcher, 2005

10 x 5 x 5 inches (25.4 x 12.7 x 12.7 cm)
White stoneware; reduction fired,
cone 10; ash glaze
PHOTO BY ARTIST

Kelsey Wheeler

Untitled, 2005

5½ x 4 x 4 inches (14 x 10.2 x 10.2 cm)
Wheel-thrown stoneware; electric fired
in oxidation, cone 6
PHOTO BY STEVE MANN

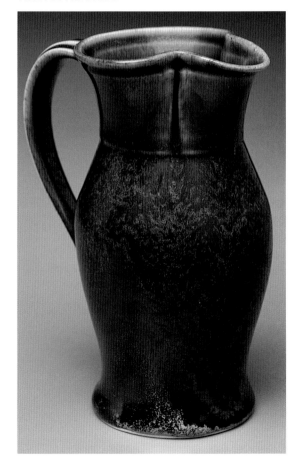

Leah Leitson

Pitcher, 2003

10 x 4½ x 7½ inches
(25.4 x 11.4 x 19 cm)
Wheel-thrown and
altered porcelain;
cone 10; salt glaze
PHOTO BY TIM BARNWELL

Jon Arsenault

> *Blue Ash Pitcher,* 1998

11 x 9 inches (27.9 x 22.9 cm)
Wheel-thrown stoneware; reduction
fired, cone 10; ash glaze
PHOTO BY NEIL PICKETT

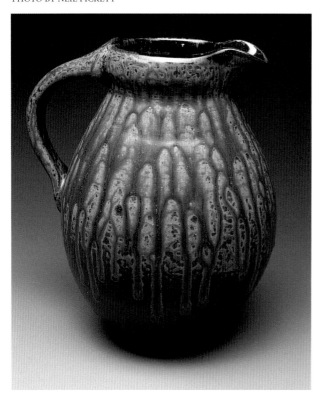

Adam Sterrett

> *Ash Glaze Pitcher,* 2005

9 x 6 x 6 inches (22.9 x 15.2 x 15.2 cm)
White stoneware; reduction fired, cone 10
PHOTO BY ARTIST

Loren Maron

| Untitled, 2005

8 x 6 x 4¼ inches (20.3 x 15.2 x 10.8 cm)
Wheel-thrown and altered porcelain;
reduction fired, cone 10; underglazes,
clear overglaze
PHOTO BY ARTIST

Georgia Tenore Jadick

Untitled, 2004

9 x 8 inches (22.9 x 20.3 cm)
Wheel-thrown stoneware; reduction fired,
cone 10; shino base glaze, layered glazes,
sponged wax resist decoration, paint
PHOTOS BY ARTIST

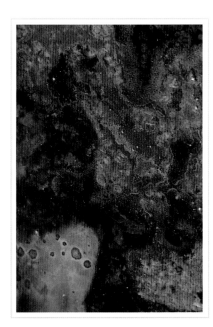

Carol Ann Wedemeyer

| Untitled, 2004

12 x 15 x 11 inches (30.5 x 38.1 x 27.9 cm)
Coil- and slab-built Arctic White
porcelain; cone 5

PHOTO BY WILFRED J. JONES

Doris Fischer-Colbrie

| *Wheeled One*, 2005

4½ x 4¾ x 1¾ inches (11.4 x 12.2 x 4.4 cm)
Wheel-thrown stoneware; reduction fired, cone 10

PHOTO BY LYNN HUNTON

Fred Kimmelstiel

Stoneware Pitcher, 2004

15 x 8 x 6 inches (38.1 x 20.3 x 15.2 cm)
Wheel-thrown stoneware; gas fired in
reduction, cone 10
PHOTO BY ARTIST

Tara Wilson

Pitcher, 2005

9 x 9 x 7 inches (22.9 x 22.9 x 17.8 cm)
Wheel-thrown and altered stoneware; wood fired
PHOTO BY ARTIST

Felicia Breen

Beetle Pitcher I, 2004

11 x 8 x 5 inches (27.9 x 20.3 x 12.7 cm)
Wheel-thrown and altered white
stoneware; salt fired, cone 10
PHOTOS BY ARTIST

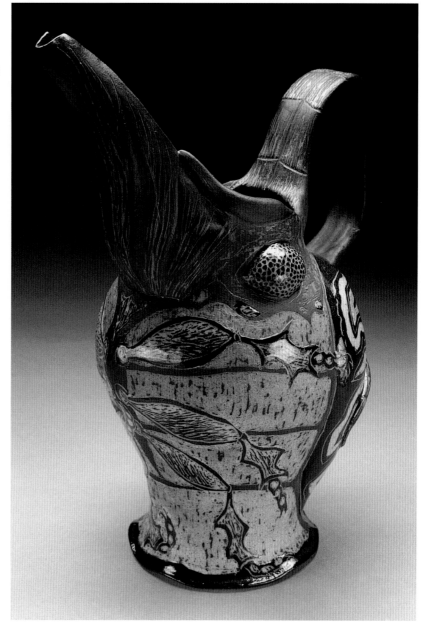

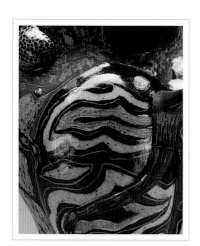

Carolina Niebres

Blue Cascade, 2004

8¼ x 7¾ x 6 inches
(21 x 19.7 x 15.2 cm)
Wheel-thrown stoneware with
pulled spout; wood fired, cone
10; wax resist, Long Beach Blue
exterior, Korean celadon
interior, rim, and spout
PHOTO BY PETRONELLA YTSMA

Glenda Taylor

Untitled, 2004

8 x 8 x 5 inches (20.3 x 20.3 x 12.7 cm)
Wheel-thrown and altered porcelain; wood
fired, cone 10; re-fired in gas kiln (reduction)
to melt ash deposits, cone 10
PHOTO BY ARTIST

Cheyenne Chapman

Table Pitcher, 2003

8 x 8 x 6 inches (20.3 x 20.3 x 15.2 cm)
Wheel-thrown and altered porcelain;
fired in oxidation with soda, cone 10
PHOTO BY ARTIST

Chris Kranz

Stoneware Pitcher, 2005

8½ x 7 inches (21.6 x 17.8 cm)
Wheel-thrown stoneware;
reduction fired, cone 12
PHOTO BY PHYLIS KING

Sandra Shaughnessy

Beak Pitcher, 2005

7 x 11 x 4 inches
(17.8 x 27.9 x 10.2 cm)
Wheel-thrown and altered
white stoneware; soda fired,
cone 10; flashing slips, glaze
PHOTO BY PETRONELLA YTSMA

Lowell T. Hoisington II

Gobbler Pitcher, 2004

10⅞ x 6 x 6 inches (27.6 x 15.2 x 15.2 cm)
Wheel-thrown stoneware; wood fired
with light salt, cone 10; flashing slip,
stain, celadon glaze

PHOTO BY ARTIST

Wayne Fuerst

Water Pitcher, 2001

15½ x 8 x 5½ inches (39.4 x 20.3 x 14 cm)
Stoneware; wood fired with salt, cone 10; trailed
shino glazes
PHOTO BY MONICA RIPLEY

Juan Granados

Twisted, 2005

8 x 8½ x 8½ inches (20.3 x 21.6 x 21.6 cm)
Wheel-thrown and altered stoneware;
reduction fired, cone 10; glaze
PHOTO BY VON VENHUIZEN

I enjoy using the wheel as an extension of my hands to alter symmetrical
forms, which allows me to play with the plasticity inherent in ceramics. —*JG*

Justin Rothshank

Slab Pitcher #5, 2004

13 x 6 x 4 inches (33 x 15.2 x 10.2 cm)
Slab-built stoneware with wheel-
thrown spout; wood fired, cone 12;
porcelain slip, shino liner glaze
PHOTO BY DAVID L. SMITH

There are engaging
qualities in Justin
Rothshank's simple
appropriation of
nature; the casual
stance, weathered
edge, and rustic glaze
of his piece suggest
tree bark, with a
branch stem as a
spout. —*TG*

Chris Archer

| *Lidded Pouring Pot,* 2005

3¼ x 3 x 4 inches
(8.3 x 7.6 x 10.2 cm)
Wheel-thrown stoneware;
reduction fired, cone 10
PHOTO BY CHARLIE FREIBURG

Christo Giles

| *Jug with Feet,* 2004

5½ x 5 x 4½ inches (14 x 13 x 11 cm)
Wheel-thrown and faceted stoneware;
wood fired, cone 11
PHOTO BY ARTIST

Linda Bourne

Untitled, 2000

9 x 9 x 2 inches (22.9 x 22.9 x 5 cm)
Hand-built, colored clay; electric fired,
cone 7; semi-matte glaze finish
PHOTO BY BILL BACHHUBER

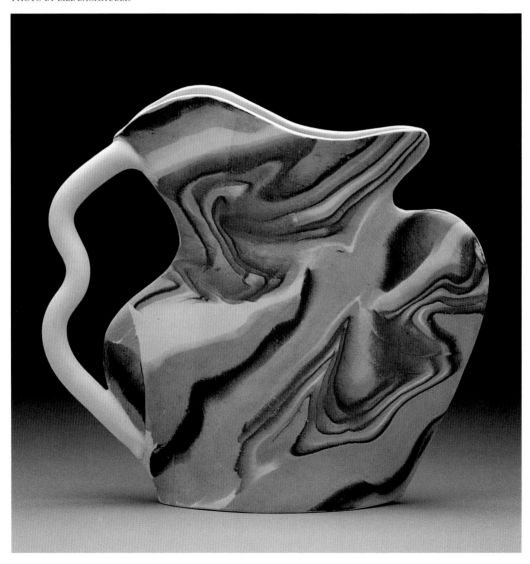

Yasmine Redding

Waterfall Pitcher, 2005

15¼ x 13 x 5½ inches (38.7 x 33 x 14 cm)
Wheel-thrown and altered stoneware; gas
fired in reduction, cone 10; spray glaze
PHOTOS BY ARTIST

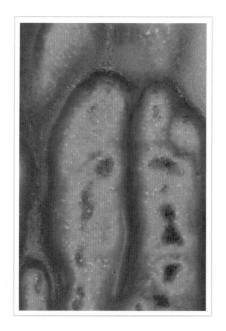

Amanda Dock

Thai-Fusion Pitcher, 2005

10¼ x 7½ x 5½ inches
(26 x 19.1 x 14 cm)
Wheel-thrown and carved stoneware;
reduction fired, cone 9

PHOTOS BY ARTIST

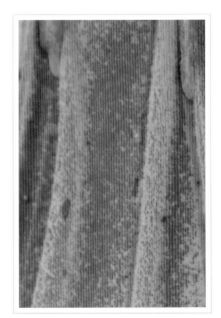

Jo Priestley

Porcelain Pitcher, 2004

10 x 7 x 5 inches (25.4 x 17.8 x 12.7 cm)
Wheel-thrown porcelain; reduction fired,
cone 10; multi-layered sprayed glazes
PHOTO BY EYE Q STUDIO

Amy Wandless

Stardust Pitcher, 2004

7 x 8½ x 7 inches (17.8 x 21.6 x 17.8 cm)
Wheel-thrown stoneware; electric fired, cone 6
PHOTO BY GREGORY A. WANDLESS

Melissa Vaughn

Almond-Shaped Pitcher, 2004

8 x 5 x 5½ inches (20.3 x 12.7 x 14 cm)
Wheel-thrown and altered stoneware;
soda fired, cone 10; multiple glazes
PHOTO BY ARTIST

Connie Christensen

Untitled, 2002

8 x 6 x 5 inches (20.3 x 15.2 x 12.7 cm)
Wheel-thrown and altered porcelain;
reduction fired, cone 10; shino glaze
PHOTO BY JOHN BONATH

Jan Stackhouse

Untitled, 2002

7 x 5 x 2½ inches (17.8 x 12.7 x 6.4 cm)
Hand-built and stamped earthenware; electric fired,
cone 02; underglazes and clear overglaze, cone 05
PHOTO BY ELIZABETH ELLINGSON
COURTESY OF HANSON-HOWARD GALLERY, ASHLAND, OREGON

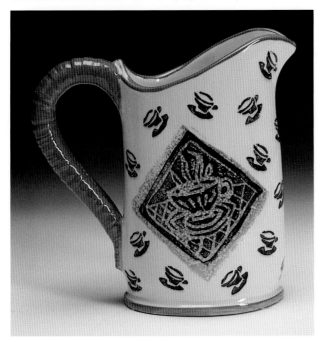

Patrick L. Dougherty

Wolf at the Door, 1994

21 x 9 inches (53.3 x 22.9 cm)
Wheel-thrown stoneware; cone 10; salt glaze
PHOTO BY JAY BACHEMIN

Craig Edwards

> *Elegant Pitcher,* 2002

12 x 6 x 6 inches (30.5 x 15.2 x 15.2 cm)
Wheel-thrown stoneware; wood fired, cone
12; flashing slip
PHOTO BY PETER LEE

Chloe Rothwell

> *Lil' Pitcher,* 2005

5½ x 5 x 3½ inches (14 x 12.7 x 8.9 cm)
Wheel-thrown and altered porcelain; soda
fired, cone 10; slip, stamps, sprigs
PHOTO BY HEATHER TINNARO

Liz Smith

| *Pitcher*, 2005

11 x 7 x 6 inches (27.9 x 17.8 x 15.2 cm)
Wheel-thrown, altered, press molded, and
carved porcelain; electric fired, cone 6;
decals and lusters, cone 019
PHOTO BY ARTIST

Tracy Shell

| *Pitcher*, 2005

8 x 5 x 4 inches (20.3 x 12.7 x 10.2 cm)
Wheel-thrown porcelain; electric
fired, cone 6
PHOTO BY ARTIST

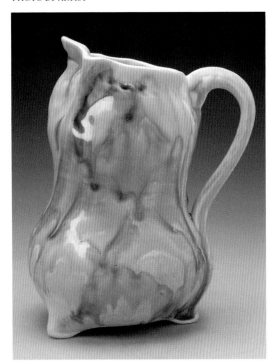

Ursula Snow Hargens

Untitled, 2004

12 x 6 x 6 inches (30.5 x 15.2 x 15.2 cm)
Wheel-thrown earthenware; electric
fired, cone 04
PHOTO BY ARTIST

Jon Arsenault

Pitcher, 2001

9 x 6 inches (22.9 x 15.2 cm)
Wheel-thrown porcelain; celadon
and temmoku glazes

Charity Davis-Woodard

Untitled, 2002

8½ x 7½ x 6½ inches (21.6 x 19 x 16.5 cm)
Wheel-thrown porcelain; wood fired in Bourry box
kiln, cone 10

Dustin Farmer

Untitled, 2005

10 x 7½ x 4 inches (25.4 x 19 x 10.2 cm)
Wheel-thrown and altered stoneware;
reduction fired, cone 10; slip trailed,
incised with celadon glaze
PHOTO BY ARTIST

Frank James Fisher

Industrial Pitcher, 2005

6 x 6 x 4 inches (15.2 x 15.2 x 10.2 cm)
Thrown and assembled porcelain;
raku fired

PHOTO BY ARTIST

Dan Anderson

Red Indian Oil Can, 2002

12 x 9 x 6½ inches (30.5 x 22.9 x 16.5 cm)
Slab-built stoneware; wood fired, 1300°F
(704°C); decal
PHOTO BY JEFF BRUCE

The tradition of making clay look like metal objects is rich and inventive; Frank James Fisher presents a faithfully replicated image, while Dan Anderson adds a nostalgic quality by means of dents and a patinated surface. —*TG*

Jay Owens

Wine Carafe, 2005

16 x 9 x 8 inches (40.6 x 22.9 x 20.3 cm)
Wheel-thrown red earthenware; electric fired,
cone 04; white slip, alkaline glaze, sgraffitto
PHOTO BY ARTIST

David Pier

> *Fluted Pitcher*, 2003

13 x 8 x 11 inches (33 x 20.3 x 27.9 cm)
Wheel-thrown and altered porcelain;
oxidation fired, cone 10
PHOTO BY ARTIST

Sharon Woodward

> *Dancing Dress*, 2005

8¾ x 6½ x 4 inches (22.2 x 16.5 x 10.2 cm)
Hand-built porcelain; transparent glaze over
underglazes; cone 06; gold lustre, cone 017
PHOTO BY ARTIST

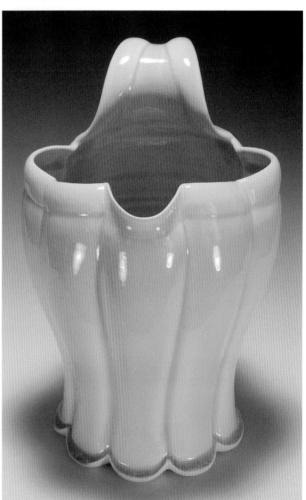

Bonita Cohn

| *Crone*, 2000

7½ x 6½ inches (19.1 x 16.5 cm)
Wheel-thrown stoneware; wood fired;
shino glaze and crackled slip
PHOTO BY ARTIST

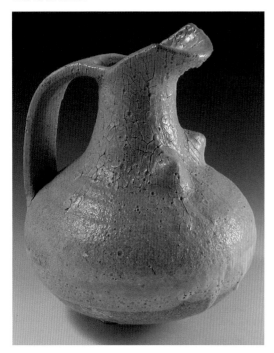

Robin Bryant

| *Tall Pitcher*, 2005

12½ x 6 inches (31.8 x 15.2 cm)
Wheel-thrown and assembled stoneware;
gas fired in reduction, cone 10
PHOTO BY ARTIST

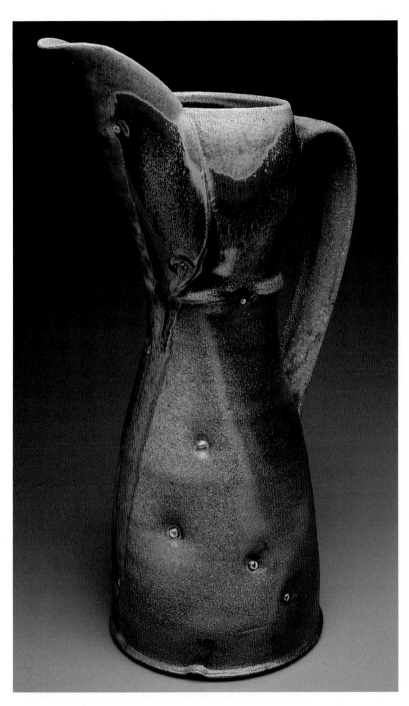

Wood-Fired Pitcher, 2004

14 x 8 x 6 inches (35.6 x 20.3 x 15.2 cm)
Wheel-thrown stoneware with slab spout
and porcelain buttons; wood fired, cone 12
PHOTO BY CHARLEY FREIBERG

Chloe Rothwell

Lil' Pitcher, 2005

5½ x 5 x 3 inches (14 x 12.7 x 7.6 cm)
Wheel-thrown and altered porcelain;
soda fired, cone 10; slips, stamps, sprigs
PHOTO BY HEATHER TINNARO

Sara Patterson

Carved Pitcher, 2004

7½ x 4½ x 4½ inches
(19 x 11.4 x 11.4 cm)
Wheel-thrown and carved
porcelain; soda fired, cone 10
PHOTO BY D. JAMES DEE

Bryan Rankin

> *Medium Pitcher,* 2004

10½ x 8 x 6½ inches (26.7 x 20.3 x 16.5 cm)
Wheel-thrown stoneware; gas fired, cone 10; glaze
PHOTO BY ARTIST

Ursula Danielewicz

> Untitled, 2003

8½ x 5¾ x 4¼ inches (21.6 x 14.6 x 10.8 cm)
Wheel-thrown stoneware; reduction, cone 10; glaze
PHOTO BY BLUEFISH STUDIOS

Dganit Moreno

Untitled, 2005

14 x 13 x 3 inches
(35.6 x 33 x 7.6 cm)
Wheel-thrown and altered
stoneware with hand-built
additions; reduction fired,
cone 9; sprayed glazes
PHOTO BY ARTIST

David Stuempfle

| *Pitcher,* 2004

15 x 7 inches (38.1 x 17.8 cm)
Wheel-turned stoneware; wood
fired; salt and ash glazes
PHOTO BY JASON DOWDLE

Marta Baillet Crane

Celadon Pitcher, 2004

7½ x 3½ x 4½ inches (19.1 x 8.9 x 11.4 cm)
Slab-built, wheel-thrown, and altered porcelain and
stoneware; reduction fired, cone 10; celadon glaze
PHOTO BY ARTIST

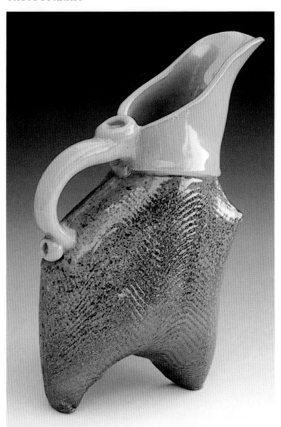

Dan Edmunds

Untitled, 2005

8 x 4 x 3 inches (20.3 x 10.2 x 7.6 cm)
Stoneware; soda fired
PHOTO BY ARTIST

Samantha Henneke

| Untitled, 2004

6 x 5 x 5 inches (15.2 x 12.7 x 12.7 cm)
Wheel-thrown porcelain; electric fired, cone 6
PHOTO BY ARTIST

Ardis A. Bourland

Big Bird Pitcher, 2001

8 x 11 x 4½ inches (20.3 x 27.9 x 11.4 cm)
Wheel-thrown white clay with hand-built
neck and handle; electric fired, cone 6;
lusters, cone 018
PHOTO BY FAREED AL MASHAT

Daniel Marinelli

Untitled, 2003

13 x 6 x 5 inches (33 x 15.2 x 12.7 cm)
Slab-built stoneware; gas fired in
reduction, cone 9
PHOTO BY ARTIST

Dale Huffman

Pitcher, 2005

10 x 7½ inches (25.4 x 19.1 cm)
Wheel-thrown stoneware; wood
fired, cone 11; natural ash glaze
PHOTO BY ARTIST

Kim Schoenberger

Untitled, 2002

24 x 11 x 11 inches (62 x 28 x 28 cm)
Wheel-thrown and coil-built clay;
electric fired, cone 4
PHOTO BY RICK HARPER

Charlie Tefft

Spotted Wren Pitcher, 2004

11 x 8½ x 6½ inches
(27.9 x 21.6 x 16.5 cm)
Wheel-thrown and altered white
stoneware; gas fired, cone 10;
oxide wash and ash glaze
PHOTO BY ARTIST

Yonghee Joo

White Flower Pitcher, 2005

7 x 8 x 6 inches (17.8 x 20.3 x 15.2 cm)
Wheel-thrown porcelain;
electric fired, cone 6
PHOTO BY D. JAMES DEE

Amelia Stamps

Sauce Boat, 2005

6½ x 6 x 6 inches (16.5 x 15.2 x 15.2 cm)
Wheel-thrown and altered white stoneware;
oxidation fired, cone 6
PHOTO BY ARTIST

Steve Stefanac

| Untitled, 2004

5 x 4 x 3 inches (12.7 x 10.2 x 7.6 cm)
Wheel-thrown porcelain; cone 10
PHOTO BY JERI HOLLISTER

Marta Baillet Crane

| *Hand Pitcher*, 2003

5½ x 5 x 3½ inches (14 x 12.7 x 8.9 cm)
Slab-built, wheel-thrown, and altered
stoneware; reduction fired, cone 10;
iron oxide glaze
PHOTO BY ARTIST

Janice Honea

Round Pitcher, 2005

12 x 9 x 9 inches (30.5 x 22.9 x 22.9 cm)
Wheel-thrown and altered stoneware;
gas fired in reduction, cone 10; shino
and sprinkled ash glaze
PHOTO BY ARTIST

Liz Smith

Pitcher, 2005

9 x 6 x 4½ inches (22.9 x 15.2 x 11.4 cm)
Wheel-thrown, altered, and press-molded
porcelain; electric fired, cone 06; decals
and lusters, cone 019
PHOTO BY ARTIST

Frank Vaculin

Green Knight Pitcher, 2005

10¼ x 10 x 6 inches (26 x 25.4 x 15.2 cm)
Wheel-thrown stoneware; gas fired, cone 10
PHOTO BY ARTIST

Ian F. Thomas

Pitcher, 2005

7 x 11¾ x 9 inches (17.8 x 29.8 x 22.9 cm)
Wheel-thrown and altered white stoneware;
reduction fired with salt and soda, cone 10
PHOTO BY ARTIST

Debra Oliva

Water Pitcher, 2005

11 x 10 x 7 inches
(27.9 x 25.4 x 17.8 cm)
Wheel-thrown and altered
porcelain; gas fired in
reduction, cone 10
PHOTO BY ARTIST

Susan D. Harris

Beaked Flacon with Crocodiles, 1996

19¼ x 12 x 4¾ inches (48.9 x 30.5 x 12 cm)
Slab-built black stoneware with thrown
additions; reduction cooled, cone 9, gold luster
PHOTO BY ROHN SOLOMON

Gary Jackson

Soda-Glazed Pitcher, 2005

11 x 9 x 6 inches (27.9 x 22.9 x 15.2 cm)
Wheel-thrown and stamped
stoneware; soda fired, cone 10;
flashing slip around rim
PHOTOS BY GUY NICOL

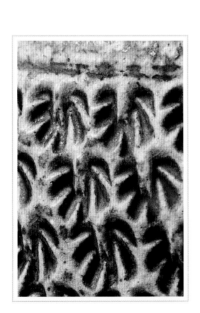

It's a control issue. When making a piece, I can control all of the
stages—throwing, trimming, and stamping. Once it's done and ready
to be soda fired, I must relinquish control and let it go. I'm intrigued
by that contrast in my work. It's like therapy. —*GJ*

Simon Levin

Combed Pitcher, 2004

9 x 6 x 7 inches (22.9 x 17.8 x 15.2 cm)
Porcelain; anagama fired, cone 9
PHOTO BY ARTIST

Robin Bryant

> *Pitcher,* 2005

8½ x 6 inches (21.6 x 15.2 cm)
Wheel-thrown stoneware; gas
fired in reduction, cone 10
PHOTO BY ARTIST

Jill Hinckley

> *Pitcher,* 2005

8½ x 4½ inches (21.6 x 11.4 cm)
Wheel-thrown stoneware; gas
fired in reduction, cone 10
PHOTO BY SUSAN WEBER

Lidded Pitcher, 2002

9 x 5½ inches (22.9 x 14 cm)
Thrown and altered stoneware;
wood fired, cone 12
PHOTO BY ARTIST

I fire the kiln with a team of friends—some potters, others not. Each
firing has a unique flavor of people and elements. So although I created
the work, a community helped bring it into its final form. This one was
from our first firing, and it's still my favorite pitcher. —JM

Kirk Mangus

> *Love Pitcher,* 2002

11½ x 10 x 9 inches
(29.2 x 25.4 x 22.9 cm)
Wheel-thrown and carved
red clay; wood fired, cone
10; white slip
PHOTO BY KEVIN OLDS

Steven Hill

Melon Pitcher, 2004

14 x 10 x 9 inches
(35.6 x 25.4 x 22.9 cm)
Wheel-thrown and altered
stoneware; single fired,
cone 10; ribbed slip design,
multiple sprayed glazes
PHOTO BY AL SURRATT

Sheila Clennell

Beaker with Saucer, 2005

4½ x 4½ x 7 inches
(11.4 x 11.4 x 17.8 cm)
Wheel-thrown stoneware with
hand-built additions; reduction
fired, cone 10; glazed
with local materials
PHOTO BY ARTIST

Debra Oliva

Pitcher, 2005

6 x 9 x 8 inches (15.2 x 22.9 x 20.3 cm)
Wheel-thrown and altered porcelain
pitcher, slab-built porcelain saucer;
gas fired in reduction, cone 10
PHOTO BY ARTIST

Wayne Fuerst

Wild Weed Water Pitcher, 2001

13 x 7½ x 6 inches (33 x 19 x 15.2 cm)
Stoneware; wood fired, cone 10; trailed glaze
PHOTO BY MONICA RIPLEY

Tyler Gulden

Table Pitcher, 2004

8 x 4½ x 5 inches (20.3 x 11.4 x 12.7 cm)
Wheel-thrown stoneware; wood fired,
cone 11; salt glaze
PHOTO BY ARTIST

Birch Frew

Untitled, 2005

7½ x 5 x 5 inches (19.1 x 12.7 x 12.7 cm)
Wheel-thrown and altered stoneware;
soda fired, cone 10
PHOTO BY ARTIST

Ben Krupka

Pitcher, 2004

12 x 7 x 6 inches
(30.5 x 17.8 x 15.2 cm)
Porcelain; wood fired, cone 10
PHOTO BY ARTIST

John Elder

Untitled, 2005

11¾ x 8½ x 8 inches (30 x 21.6 x 20.3 cm)
Thrown stoneware, slip; salt fired, cone 10;
brush decoration

PHOTO BY ROBERT NELSON

I want my decoration on the
pitcher to encourage pouring
from the pot. —*JE*

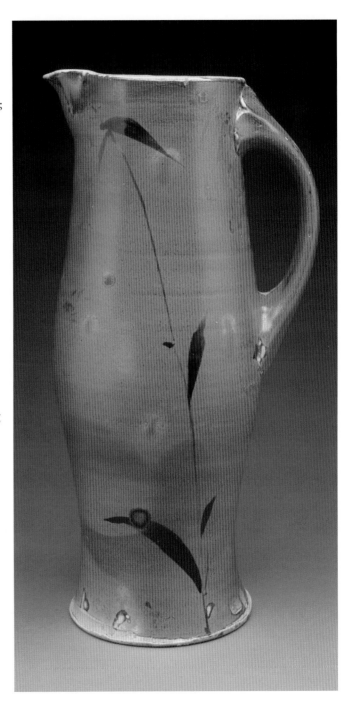

Eleanor Pugh
Hal Pugh

| Untitled, 2005

9½ x 6½ inches (24.1 x 16.5 cm)
Wheel-thrown redware; oxidation fired,
cone 02; slip decoration
PHOTO BY KENNETH AND ZACH ORR

Some potters are
happiest studying a
favorite cultural style
and honoring that
tradition with either
faithful replication or by
working in that style.
Eleanor and Hal Pugh
present a covered jug
that clings closely to
ancestral roots. —TG

Larry Pennington

Untitled, 2003

7½ x 9 x 6½ inches (19 x 22.9 x 16.5 cm)
Terra cotta; low fired, cone 04; underglazes
PHOTO BY ARTIST

Brad Tucker

Untitled, 2004

12½ x 7 inches (31.8 x 17.8 cm)
Wheel-thrown stoneware; gas fired in
reduction, cone 10; ash glazes
PHOTO BY SETH TICE-LEWIS

Paul Donnelly

Pitcher, 2005

10¼ x 8½ x 5¾ inches (26 x 21.6 x 14.6 cm)
Wheel-thrown and hand-decorated
porcelain; reduction fired, cone 10;
celadon glaze
PHOTO BY JOHN CARLANO

Paul Donnelly and Brad Tucker present two diverging approaches to the
old problem of making a spout that looks good and pours well. —*TG*

Elizabeth Kendall

Water Pitcher, 2005

9 x 5 x 3 inches (22.9 x 12.7 x 7.6 cm)
Slab-built porcelain; gas fired in
Minnesota flat-top car kiln, cone 10;
Oribe variation; rim dipped in glass frit
PHOTO BY ARTIST

The glass frit on
the rim caused the
underlying glaze to
melt, foam, and flow.
It's as if the liquid
in the pitcher has
splashed out and
down the sides. —*EK*

Posey Bacopoulos

| *Beaked Pitcher*, 2004

7 x 8 x 3½ inches (17.8 x 20.3 x 8.9 cm)
Wheel-thrown, altered, and assembled
terra cotta; electric fired, cone 04;
majolica glazes

PHOTO BY KEVIN NOBLE

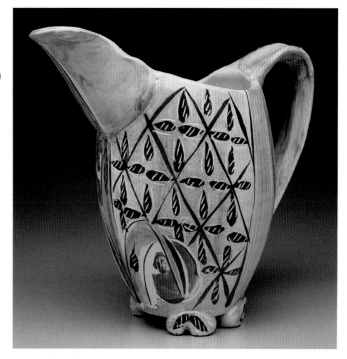

Theresa M. Gresham

| *Blue Pitcher*, 2005

5 x 6¼ x 4¼ inches
(12.7 x 15.9 x 10.8 cm)
Wheel-thrown and
altered porcelain;
electric fired, cone 6

PHOTO BY PETER LENZO

George Handy

Fluted Canteen, 2005

11 x 7 x 7 inches (27.9 x 17.8 x 17.8 cm)
Wheel-thrown and altered porcelain;
oxidation fired, cone 6; celadon glaze,
low-fire stains, oxide washes

PHOTO BY TIM BARNWELL

Tim Ludwig

Pitcher with Peony, 2004

23 x 16 x 14 inches (58.4 x 40.6 x 35.6 cm)
Wheel-thrown earthenware; electric fired,
cone 05; Mason stains, slips
PHOTO BY RANDY SMITH

The accomplished surface treatments of Tim Ludwig and George Handy
each demonstrate that, with practiced skill, electric kilns offer a unique
range of possibility. —*TG*

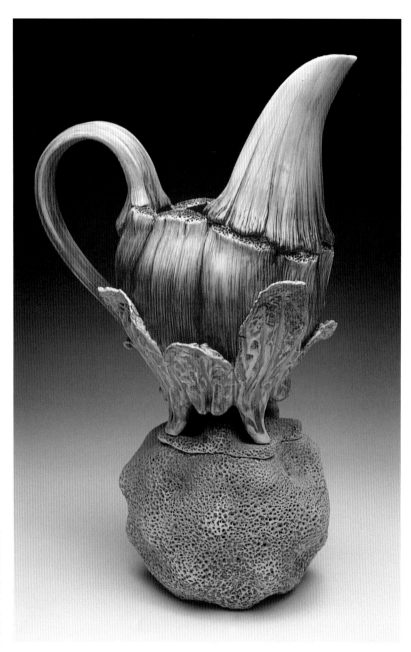

Bonnie Seeman

Creamer & Sugar Container, 2001

10 x 6 x 5 inches (25.4 x 15.2 x 12.7 cm)
Wheel-thrown and hand-built porcelain;
electric fired, cone 10
PHOTO BY ARTIST

Rachel Bleil

| *Pitcher and Drawer,* 2005

13¼ x 7¼ x 5 inches (33.7 x 18.4 x 12.7 cm)
Wheel-thrown, hand-built, and press-molded
white earthenware; electric fired, cone 04;
terra sigillata, stains, underglazes, glazes
PHOTOS BY ARTIST

This pitcher was designed primarily to be overly ornate, but also
to contain a drawer for packaged sugar substitutes. —*RB*

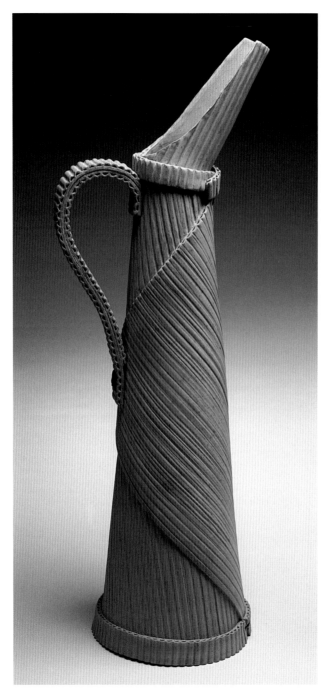

Lorraine Sutter

| Untitled, 2005

23½ x 8¼ x 6¾ inches (60 x 21 x 17 cm)
Corrugated, textured, and slab-built
porcelain; electric fired, cone 6;
wire additions
PHOTOS BY AK PHOTOS

Charity Davis-Woodard

Untitled, 2001

11 x 8½ x 6 inches (27.9 x 21.6 x 15.2 cm)
Wheel-thrown porcelain; wood fired in
anagama kiln, cone 11
PHOTO BY JEFF BRUCE

Charity Davis-Woodard
has balanced the belly's
swell with a foot and
neck of fairly equal
proportion, resulting
in a secure, infinitely
usable pitcher. —TG

Dale Huffman

Pitcher, 2005

10½ x 7¾ inches (26.7 x 19.7 cm)
Wheel-thrown stoneware; wood fired, cone 9
PHOTO BY ARTIST

Marsha Karagheusian

Copper Blues, 2005

10½ x 6½ x 5 inches (26.7 x 16.5 x 12.7 cm)
Hand-built and textured earthenware; electric
fired, cone 06; multiple stains; pit fired in
straw and sawdust
PHOTO BY MEL MITTERMILLER

With the life-sustaining
fluids that flow from
it, the pitcher nurtures
the vitality of human
existence and cradles
the spirit of life. —*MK*

Hide Sadohara

| *Pitcher,* 1995

10 x 6 x 6 inches (25.4 x 15.2 x 15.2 cm)
Thrown porcelain; reduction fired, cone 10
PHOTO BY ARTIST

From its raised foot
to its rolling lip,
Hide Sadohara's
Pitcher is as fluid as
any beverage it will
ever contain. —*TG*

Phil Kreider

Satin White Pitcher, 2005

8 x 6 x 4½ inches (20.3 x 15.2 x 11.4 cm)
Wheel-thrown, darted, and stretched
stoneware; soda fired, cone 10
PHOTOS BY ARTIST

Craig Edwards

Picturesque, 2005

11 x 9 x 4 inches (27.9 x 22.9 x 10.2 cm)
Slab-built stoneware; electric fired,
cone 8; ash glaze
PHOTO BY PETER LEE

Luke Sheets

Ribbon Pitcher, 2002

8½ x 5 x 5 inches (21.6 x 12.7 x 12.7 cm)
Altered, carved, and wheel-thrown
porcelain; gas fired in reduction, cone 10
PHOTO BY ARTIST

Bill Gossman

Pitcher with Red Spot, 2002

12 x 6 x 6 inches (30.5 x 15.2 x 15.2 cm)
Wheel-thrown stoneware; wood fired,
cone 11; textured; salt glaze
PHOTO BY PETER LEE

Luke Sheets

Green and Blue Pitcher, 2000

8½ x 5 x 5 inches (21.6 x 12.7 x 12.7 cm)
Wheel-thrown and altered stoneware; soda
fired, cone 10
PHOTO BY ARTIST

Blair Clemo

Pitcher with Yellow Roses, 2005

9 x 8 x 5 inches (22.9 x 20.3 x 12.7 cm)
Wheel-thrown porcelain; oxidation fired, cone
7; inlaid slip, stamped underglaze, decals
PHOTO BY CHRIS AUTIO

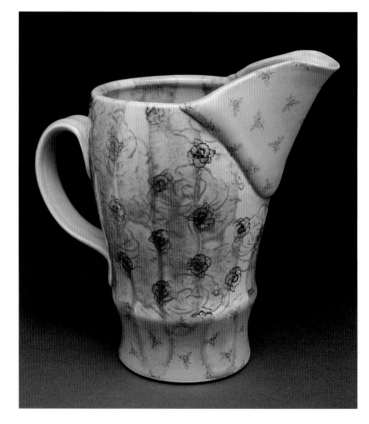

Josh Copus

| *Medieval English Jug,* 2004

10 x 5 x 4 inches (25.4 x 12.7 x 10.2 cm)
Wheel-thrown stoneware; wood fired,
cone 11; ash glaze
PHOTO BY ARTIST

Josh Copus presents a lean
form: its handle is logically
placed as a bridge between
two horizontal protrusions,
and, though slender, this
pitcher achieves its grace by
means of its substantial
height. —*TG*

Susan Robertson

Stoney Plains Birches #2, 1991

9¾ x 6¾ inches (24.8 x 17.1 cm)
Slab-built porcelain; electric fired,
cone 6; sprigged, airbrushed, and
hand-painted polychromatic
underglaze; glaze

PHOTOS BY GARY ROBINS

Renee A. McArty

Nature, 2005

14 x 6 x 9 inches
(35.6 x 15.2 x 22.9 cm)
Slab-built and darted
white stoneware; low-fire
glazes, cone 04
PHOTO BY ARTIST

Lorna Meaden

Untitled, 2005

9 x 8 x 4½ inches
(22.9 x 20.3 x 11.4 cm)
Porcelain; soda fired, cone 10
PHOTO BY BRAD SCHWIEGER

Nick Ramey

Untitled, 2005

8½ x 5 x 4½ inches (21.6 x 12.7 x 11.4 cm)
Wheel-thrown and altered stoneware;
wood fired with soda, cone 11; underglaze,
natural ash glaze
PHOTOS BY ARTIST

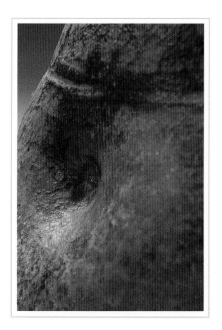

Kathy Steinsberger

Secret Garden in Pittsburgh, 2003

5½ x 6 x 4½ inches (14 x 15.2 x 11.4 cm)
Red earthenware; low fired; underglazes and glaze
PHOTO BY TOM MILLS

Barbi Lock Lee

Pitcher with Orange-Bellied Parrot, 2004

4½ x 5¼ x 3 inches (11.4 x 13.3 x 7.6 cm)
Slip-cast earthenware; electric fired,
cone 02; underglazes
PHOTOS BY MICHEL BROUET

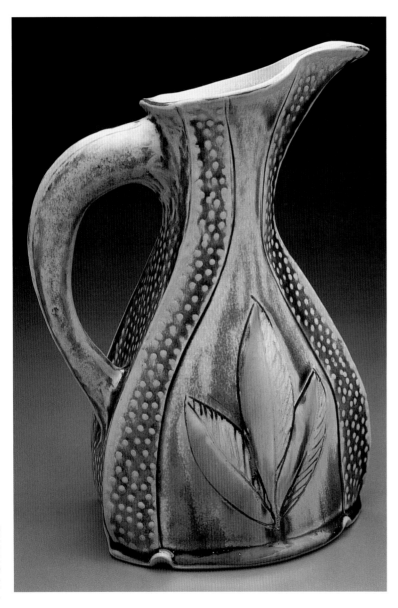

Barbara Knutson

| *Leaf Pitcher*, 2003

10 x 6 x 4 inches (25.4 x 15.2 x 10.2 cm)
Hand-built white stoneware; propane
fired in reduction, cone 10; rutile slip
brushed over glaze

PHOTO BY CHARLIE FREIBERG

Nicholas Seidner

Pitcher, 2004

11 x 6 x 6 inches (27.9 x 15.2 x 15.2 cm)
Wheel-thrown stoneware; salt and soda
fired in gas, cone 10; thrown and
attached spout
PHOTO BY ARTIST

Note the noble
characteristics present
in Nicholas Seidner's
pitcher: the weathered
glaze, the wide foot
and generous belly,
the handle and spout
that spring from
the lip. —*TG*

Les G. Laidlaw

Bird Pitcher, 2005

17 x 7 x 10 inches (43.2 x 17.8 x 25.4 cm)
Wheel-thrown stoneware; electric
fired, cone 6
PHOTO BY ARTIST

Les G. Laidlaw's pitcher
echoes natural leaf
references, but his
approach is lean, spare,
and condensed. —*TG*

JoAnne L. Wilson

Untitled, 2004

11 x 5 x 5 inches (27.9 x 12.7 x 12.7 cm)
Wheel-thrown faceted stoneware; wood
fired, cone 11; celadon glaze (interior),
fly-ash glazes (exterior)
PHOTO BY MATTHEW K. WILSON

Kathryne Koop

Untitled, 2003

13 x 10 x 6 inches (33 x 25.4 x 15.2 cm)
Wheel-thrown porcelain; gas fired in
reduction, cone 11
PHOTO BY BRUCE SPIELMAN

Jill Hinckley

Two Pitchers, 2004

Left: 8½ x 6 inches (21.6 x 15.2 cm); Right: 8½ x 5¾ inches (21.6 x 14.6)
Wheel-thrown and altered porcelain; gas fired in reduction, cone 10
PHOTOS BY ARTIST

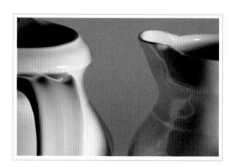

Christine Purdy

Tall Heron Jug, 2004

17¾ x 5 ¹⁵⁄₁₆ x 7⅛ inches (45 x 15 x 18 cm)
Slab-built Earthstone clay; wood fired,
2372°F (1300°C); matte crystalline glaze
with zinc and barium
PHOTO BY ARTIST

Randal Fedje

Pitcher, 2005

11¹³⁄₁₆ x 7¹⁄₁₆ inches (30 x 18 cm)
Wheel-thrown stoneware; electric fired,
cone 10; underglaze slip decoration
PHOTO BY DON HILDRED

Crystalline Pitcher, 2005

9⅛ x 6⅝ x 4¾ inches (23 x 17 x 12 cm)
Wheel-thrown porcelain; electric fired, cone 7
PHOTOS BY ARTIST

Cynthia Bringle

Covered Pitcher with Bird, 2005

11 x 8½ x 7 inches (27.9 x 21.6 x 17.8 cm)
Wheel-thrown stoneware with added
spout; gas fired, cone 10
PHOTO BY TOM MILLS

Toucan Pitcher, 2003

13 x 10 x 6½ inches (33 x 25.4 x 16.5 cm)
Slab- and coil-built stoneware; reduction
fired with salt and soda, cone 10
PHOTO BY OMS PHOTOGRAPHY

Maureen Mills

Amber Stoneware Pitcher, 2003

8 x 4 x 3 inches (20.3 x 10.2 x 7.6 cm)
Wheel-thrown and altered stoneware; gas
fired in reduction, cone 10; slip trailing
PHOTO BY CHARLEY FREIBERG

Maureen Mills
incorporates the lip
of her pitcher into a
kind of sleeve, and
manages to sprinkle
slip-trailed pattern
across the form
without undue
fussiness or static
regularity. —*TG*

Samuel S. Dowd

Untitled, 2005

8¾ x 8 x 2¼ inches (22.2 x 20.3 x 5.7 cm)
Slip-cast and altered stoneware; electric
fired, cone 6; stains and glazes, cone 06
PHOTO BY ARTIST

There's an old saying, "Every kettle has a cover." Something similar could be said for pitchers and their appropriate functions. Samuel S. Dowd's geometric hand-built construction appears well suited to display a flower garden bouquet. —TG

Thomas Perry

Zebra Pitcher, 2004

13 x 7 x 5 inches (33 x 17.8 x 12.7 cm)
Slab-built and inlaid porcelain; electric
fired, cones 9 to 10
PHOTO BY RICK WELLS

Bryan Rankin

▍ *Medium Pitcher*, 2004

8½ x 8 x 6 inches (21.6 x 20.3 x 15.2 cm)
Wheel-thrown stoneware; gas fired, cone 10;
ash glazes
PHOTO BY ARTIST

Samantha Henneke

▍ Untitled, 2004

8 x 6 x 6 inches (20.3 x 15.2 x 15.2 cm)
Wheel-thrown porcelain; electric fired, cone 6
PHOTO BY ARTIST

Tracy Shell

Pitcher, 2005

6½ x 5 x 4 inches (16.5 x 12.7 x 10.2 cm)
Wheel-thrown porcelain; electric fired, cone 6
PHOTO BY ARTIST

Tracy Shell's choice of pastel colors and sugary glaze surfaces imbues her pitcher with confectionary allusions. —*TG*

Clarice Ann Dorst

Blossom Pitcher, 2003

10½ x 6½ x 6 inches
(26.7 x 16.5 x 15.2 cm)
Wheel-thrown and
constructed stoneware;
gas fired in reduction, cone 10
PHOTO BY ARTIST

Tara Wilson

Pitcher, 2004

9 x 6 x 4 inches (22.9 x 15.2 x 10.2 cm)
Thrown and altered stoneware; salt and
soda fired
PHOTO BY ARTIST

Negative space, particularly within the handle enclosure, is a key visual element in any pitcher. In Tara Wilson's piece, this space plays off the entire asymmetric profile. —*TG*

Brad Schwieger

Cut Pitcher, 2005

13 x 9 x 7 inches (33 x 22.9 x 17.8 cm)
Wheel-thrown stoneware; soda fired,
cone 10; slip and glazes
PHOTO BY ARTIST

Liz de Beer

| Untitled, 2003

11½ inches (29.2 cm)
Wheel-thrown porcelain; electric
fired, cone 06; Celadon Green, cone 6;
multi-fired Shiny Blue, cone 03
PHOTO BY JAN DE BEER

Brad McLemore

| *Pitcher*, 2005

10½ x 6 x 5 inches (26.7 x 15.2 x 12.7 cm)
Wheel-thrown stoneware; soda fired in
reduction, cone 10; glaze
PHOTO BY ARTIST

Vladimir Groh

> *Pitcher 1,* 2005

5⅞ x 2¾ x 2¾ inches (15 x 7 x 7 cm)
Slip-cast porcelain; gas fired, 2408°F
(1320°C); overglaze
PHOTO BY ARTIST

ACKNOWLEDGMENTS

It is an honor to publish the work of so many fine artists in this, the fifth in Lark Books' "500" series of contemporary ceramic work. The book would not have been possible without Roan Mountain (North Carolina) potter Terry Gess's considerable talents as juror and clay sage. Also vital to this effort, as they handled the worldwide flood of more than 4,000 entries, were Lark's editorial stalwarts Rebecca Guthrie, Nathalie Mornu, Rosemary Kast, Delores Gosnell, and Dawn Dillingham. They were ably assisted by interns David Squires and Metta L. Pry. The book's design was guided by the metaphysics-minded Kristi Pfeffer, who was aided by her steady and true art colleagues Shannon Yokeley and Jeff Hamilton, as well as layout maven Jackie Kerr.

Finally, we here at Lark salute these outstanding potters for their marvelous work, which here presents a singular moment—a snapshot, if you will—of today's clay.

—*Suzanne J. E. Tourtillott*

Terry Gess is a studio potter in Bakersville, North Carolina. He earned his BFA from the Cleveland Institute of Art as well as an MFA from Southern Illinois University at Edwardsville. He has been the recipient of numerous awards, including the three-year Artist Residency at Penland School of Crafts, and the North Carolina Arts Council Residency at La Napoule, France. Further awards have included participation in International Ceramic Symposiums in Finland and The People's Republic of China. Terry is the author of several published essays and articles, and he lectures and teaches workshops widely.

IMAGE CREDITS
Cover: Cheyenne Chapman, *Table Pitcher*, 2003
Back cover: Monica Ripley, *Water Pitcher*, 2004; Rachel Berg, Untitled, 2004; Debra E. Sloan, *Dog Pitcher*, 2005
Spine: Ben Jensen, *Pitcher with Waves*, 2005
Front flap: Mark Fitzgerald, Untitled, 2004
Back flap: Anne Fallis Elliot, *Side Handle Pitcher on a Tray*, 2003
Page 2: Simon Levin, *Combed Pitcher*, 2004
Title page: Posey Bacopoulos, *Gravy Pitcher*, 2005
Page 4: Frank James Fisher, *Newspaper Pitcher*, 2005
Contents page, clockwise from upper left: Jeff Brown, *Carafe*, 2003; Dan Edmunds, Untitled, 2005; Nicole Copel, Untitled, 2004